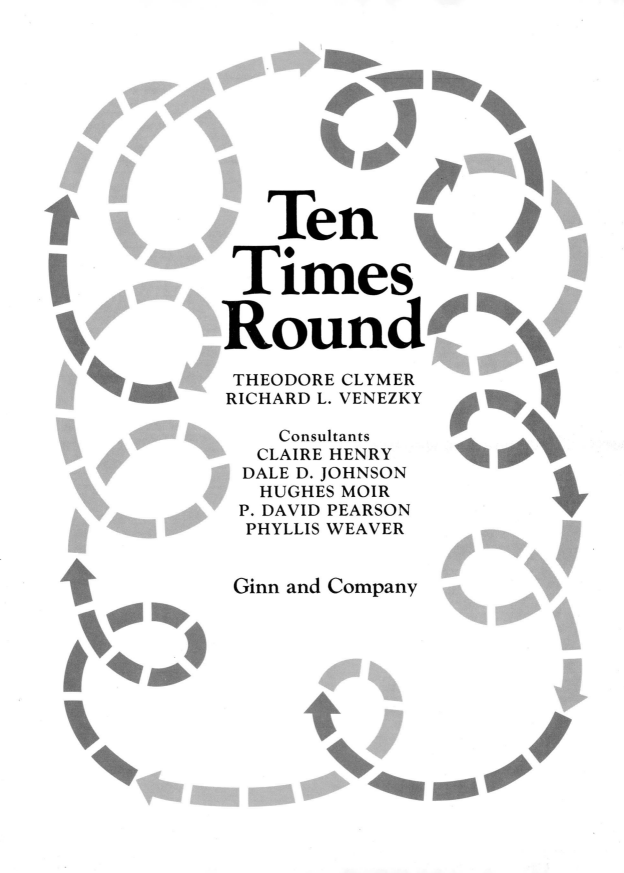

Ten Times Round

THEODORE CLYMER
RICHARD L. VENEZKY

Consultants
CLAIRE HENRY
DALE D. JOHNSON
HUGHES MOIR
P. DAVID PEARSON
PHYLLIS WEAVER

Ginn and Company

0-663-38896-1

Acknowledgements: Grateful acknowledgement is made to the following publishers, authors, and agents for permission to use and adapt copyrighted material:

Coward, McCann & Geoghegan, Inc., for "Animal Homes" by Sally Cartwright. Adapted by permission of Coward, McCann & Geoghegan, Inc. from *The Animal Homes* by Sally Cartwright. Copyright © 1973 by Sally Cartwright.

Doubleday & Company, Inc., for "Once Upon a Tree," which is an excerpt from "Where Knock is Open Wide" by Theodore Roethke, copyright 1950 by Theodore Roethke. From the book *The Collected Poems of Theodore Roethke.* Reprinted by permission of Doubleday & Company, Inc.

Elsevier-Dutton Publishing Co., Inc., for the poem "Before You Came This Way" from *Before You Came This Way* by Byrd Baylor and Tom Bahti. Text copyright © 1969 by Byrd Baylor. Reproduced by permission of the publisher, E. P. Dutton.

Follett Publishing Company for "Food's on the Table" adapted from *All-of-a-Kind Family Uptown* by Sydney Taylor. Copyright © 1958 by Sydney Taylor. Used by permission of Follett Publishing Company.

Harper & Row, Publishers, Inc., for selected illustrations from and an adaptation of the complete text of *Fossils Tell of Long Ago*, written and illustrated by Aliki. Copyright © 1972 by Aliki Brandenberg. A Let's-Read-And-Find-Out Book. By permission of Thomas Y. Crowell, Publishers. Also for an adaptation of the complete text of *Bats in the Dark* by John Kaufmann. Copyright © 1972 by John Kaufmann. A Let's-Read-And-Find-Out Book. By permission of Thomas Y. Crowell, Publishers. Also for an adaptation of the complete text of *The Rice Bowl Pet* by Patricia Miles Martin. Text copyright © 1962 by Patricia Miles Martin. By permission of Thomas Y. Crowell, Publishers.

Houghton Mifflin Company for "Tools for Swimming," adapted from *Benjamin Franklin: The First Great American,* by John Tottle. Copyright 1958 by Houghton Mifflin Company. Reprinted by permission of the publisher, Houghton Mifflin Company.

Macmillan Publishing Co., Inc., for "The Clay Horse" by Martha Goldberg. Adapted with permission of Macmillan Publishing Co., Inc. from *Big Horse, Little Horse* by Martha Goldberg.

Copyright © 1960 by Martha Goldberg. Also for "Elisabeth, the Treasure Hunter," with selected illustrations, by Felice Holman. Adapted with permission of Macmillan Publishing Co., Inc. from *Elisabeth, the Treasure Hunter* by Felice Holman. Copyright © Felice Holman, 1964.

Random House, Inc., for "The Queen Who Couldn't Bake Gingerbread" by Dorothy Van Woerkom. Adapted by permission of Alfred A. Knopf, Inc. from *The Queen Who Couldn't Bake Gingerbread,* by Dorothy Van Woerkom. Copyright © 1975 by Dorothy Van Woerkom.

Charles Scribner's Sons for "Bear Mouse in Winter," a condensation of *Bear Mouse* by Berniece Freschet. Text copyright © 1973 by Berniece Freschet. Reprinted by permission of Charles Scribner's Sons.

Evelyn Singer Agency, Inc., for "Animal Homes" adapted from *The Animal Homes* by Sally Cartwright. Copyright © 1973 by Sally Cartwright. By permission of the author's agent.

Viking Penguin Inc. for a slightly abridged version of *Gillespie and the Guards* by Benjamin Elkin. Text copyright © 1956 by Benjamin Elkin and James Daugherty. Reprinted by permission of Viking Penguin Inc.

Jan Andrews for the adaptation of her story "The Very Last First." Appeared originally in *Cricket* Magazine, February 1979. Used by permission of the author.

A & C Black (Publishers) Ltd, London, for the adapted text & art of *Fossils Tell of Long Ago* by Aliki. Also for the adapted text of *Bats in the Dark* by John Kaufmann. Both used by permission of the British publisher.

Curtis Brown, Ltd., New York, for "Gabrielle and Selena," adapted from *Gabrielle and Selena* by Peter Desbarats. Reprinted by permission of Curtis Brown, Ltd. Copyright © 1968 by Peter Desbarats. Also for "Great-aunt Pippa's Pepperoni Pizza," adapted from *Monsters, Ghoulies and Creepy Creatures - Fantastic Stories and Poems* selected by Lee Bennett Hopkins. Reprinted by permission of Curtis Brown, Ltd. Copyright © 1977 by Lee Bennett Hopkins.

Creative Education, Inc., for the adaptation of *Dream Dancer* by Evelyn Bolton. Copyright © 1974 by Creative Education. Used by permission of the publisher.

Ellis Credle for "The Goat That Went to School," Parts 1 and 2, adapted from her book *Tall Tales from the High Hills.* © 1957, by Ellis Credle. Appeared originally in *Story Parade.* Used by permission of the author.

Faber and Faber Limited, London, for "Once Upon a Tree," which is an excerpt from "Where Knock Is Open Wide" by Theodore Roethke.

(Continued on page 334)

Contents

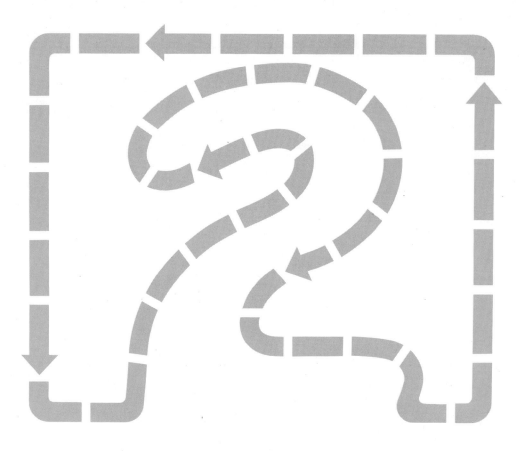

4

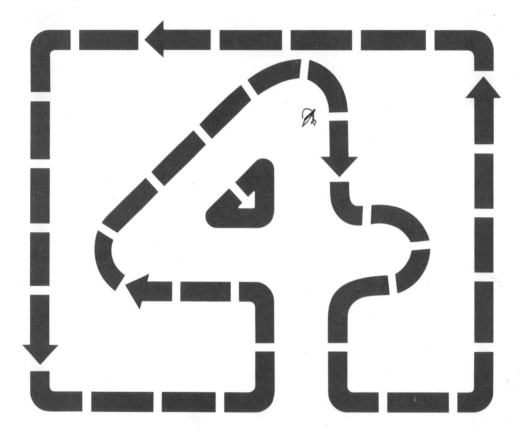

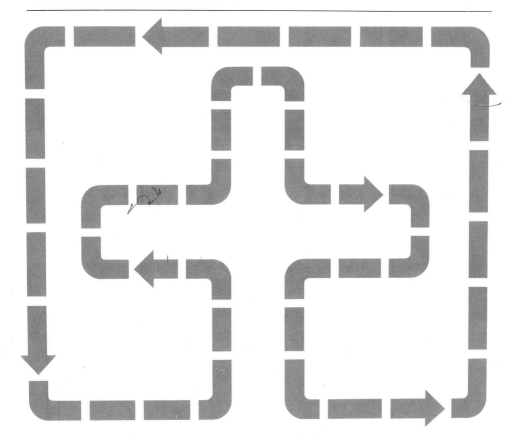

Book-length Story

Open Do

Some doors open in. Ella opens the door of her aunt's apartment and gets a surprise. Doors open for Teresa, and she finds herself in the long hallways of a busy airport. She tries to help her family, then has to help herself.

Sometimes you open a door to go out. Big garage doors swing open when the fire team goes to put out a fire. The people on the fire team go out to help others. Eric and Jon open their doors to go fishing for the day.

Turning a page can be like opening a door. There can be a surprise on the other side of a page, or a door. So turn the page, and read these stories about people.

Ors

9

We use many phrases to make others feel welcome. "The door is open—come right in." "Be my guest." "Help yourself!" The title of this story is another such phrase, so "Help yourself—food's on the table!"

Food's on the Table

SYDNEY TAYLOR

Ella glanced at the slip of paper in her hand. "We want 725—it must be the next block."

The girls—Ella, Henny, Sarah, Charlotte, and Gertie—and little Charlie were going to their aunt's new apartment for supper. Their mother would meet them there later.

"Now," Ella said, "let's see. There is 721—723. Here it is—725. It's a nice-looking building."

Ella glanced at the paper again. "Third floor, apartment four!"

The children trooped after her up the stoop. "Shouldn't we ring the bell first?" asked Gertie.

"The buzzer's out of order," Ella replied. "Lena said we should go right up."

"Come on, Charlie, we'll swing you up the stairs," said Henny. "Take his other hand, Sarah."

Whooping with delight, Charlie was swung up the stairs. His feet never once touched the ground.

Henny tapped on apartment door number four. There was no answer. She tapped again, louder, but still there was no answer.

"That's strange," Ella said. "I know Lena is expecting us." She touched the doorknob. "The door's open."

"I guess she means for us to come right in," Henny said.

"Maybe she can't hear us," suggested Gertie.

"Well, let's go in and find out," Ella said, pushing open the door. "Lena! Lena, we're here!"

There was no reply.

They went through a small hall. It led into a big square kitchen. "Is anybody home?" Charlotte shouted.

The house was still. The children looked around, not knowing quite what to do.

"Anyway, the food's on the table," Henny said cheerfully. Her eyes feasted on a slab of homemade corned beef. "Mmm, doesn't that look good!"

"And potato salad! And cole slaw!" rejoiced Gertie. "Lena sure knows what we like."

"Look, Ella," Sarah pointed. "There's a note on the table." She picked it up and read aloud: "I had to go shopping. I'll be a little late. Don't wait for me. Go ahead and eat."

"Well, that's that," remarked Henny. "Let's eat."

"Oh, I don't think that would be very nice," Ella said. "Let's wait a little while."

"We could finish setting the table," suggested Sarah. "Lena must have been in an awful hurry. There are no plates, and just three settings of silver."

13

Henny opened the door of the pantry. "These are pretty dishes. Lena must have gotten a new set."

"These kitchen chairs are pretty, too," added Charlotte.

"Uncle Hyman must be doing well," Ella said.

In no time at all, the table was properly set. Now all that was left to do was to sit around and wait.

"I'm glad Lena has moved near to us," Gertie remarked. "Now we'll be able to see her so much more often."

"I'm hungry!" Charlie piped up. "I want to eat!"

"We have to wait till Lena comes, Charlie," Ella told him.

"But I'm hungry now!"

"We're all hungry, Charlie," said Henny. "Couldn't you wait just a tiny bit longer?"

"All right," Charlie said, pouting.

"I wonder how long Mama will be," Ella said. "I hope she gets here in time to eat with us."

"Oh, where is that Lena? I'm hungry!" Henny cried.

"So am I," Charlotte chimed in. "Say, Ella, couldn't we at least get started? Lena said we should."

"I don't know. It's not very polite. What do you think, Henny?"

"She left a note, didn't she? So I say we should

eat."

"There isn't very much of this stuff, so let's be careful." Ella spooned out the salad.

"Maybe it's because Lena's not used to cooking for a big mob like us," put in Charlotte. "There are only two of them."

"That's so, but I don't quite understand it," Ella said. She finished slicing the meat. "You know how she and Uncle Hyman are about food. Usually their table groans with all they serve. Well, help yourselves. I'll put on the water for tea."

"I want another corned beef sandwich," Charlie said.

"It's a lucky thing corned beef comes in one big piece. Otherwise we wouldn't have had enough of that either."

"Well, take it easy. Let that be the last," Ella said. "There's hardly anything left."

Someone was at the door. It opened, and a short, stout woman came in. Her arms were piled high with shopping bags. "Hello," she said, looking around.

The girls all turned and looked at the newcomer. "My aunt hasn't gotten back yet," Ella offered.

The woman looked puzzled. She gave a quick glance at the door. "You're expecting your aunt?"

"Yes," Henny replied. "Don't go away. She should

be here any minute. Here, let me help you with the packages."

"Thank you, but . . ."

Her packages were set safely on a chair. The woman folded her arms and looked at the children. "Now tell me, who are you?"

"We're the nieces and this is the nephew, Charlie," Ella told her.

The woman smiled and gave a nod. "That's nice. I'm pleased to meet you." Then her eyes fell on the table. A look of dismay passed over her face. "Oh, my goodness! I see you ate up the whole supper!"

"Were you invited, too?" Ella asked.

"Who's invited? The supper was for my husband and my son."

"Good gracious!" Henny cried. "How many people were supposed to eat here tonight?"

"My dear child, you don't understand. The supper was just for the three of us—my husband, my son, and me. After all, this is my apartment."

There was a moment of stunned silence. None of the children could think of anything to say. Finally it was Ella who found her voice. "Your apartment! This is your apartment?"

"Yes," the woman told her.

"But isn't this apartment four?" added Sarah.

The woman smiled. "Yes."

"And isn't this the third floor?" Ella asked.

"No. The third floor is downstairs underneath my apartment. This is the fourth floor."

"But how could that be?" Ella asked. "We walked up three flights."

"Oh, I see." The woman nodded her head. "You didn't know that the ground floor is called the first floor. You should have walked up only two flights more."

Ella could feel her cheeks turning scarlet. "Oh, we made such a dreadful mistake! I'm terribly sorry! You see, we thought we were in our aunt's apartment. Then we read the note . . . ," she ended lamely.

The woman shrugged her shoulders and chuckled. "Well, it's all right. What's done is done. Don't worry. A mistake can happen."

"But we ate up all your food!" Henny said.

"Well, as long as you enjoyed it," the woman replied. By now she seemed rather amused.

Slowly the children started edging toward the door. Gertie and Charlotte were the first to slip out. They stood around in the doorway, wanting to get away yet unable to do so.

"We didn't know . . . ," Sarah finished.

As if out of nowhere, Mama and Lena appeared.

"What's the matter?" Mama demanded. "Where have you been?"

Lena interrupted. "I was all ready to call the police. I kept opening the door to see if you were coming. Then we heard your voices, and we came upstairs to see. What are you doing here?"

Everybody began talking at once.

"Oh, Mama!"

"Oh, Lena!"

"It was all a big mistake!"

"We thought this was your apartment, Lena!"

"Quiet a minute!" Mama ordered. "I don't know

19

what you're saying! Ella, tell me what happened."

Ella looked embarrassed. "Well, Mama, I know it sounds dreadful. First we went into this lady's apartment. Then we ate up her supper."

"The whole supper, Mama!" Gertie burst in. "It was supposed to be for her husband and her son, too."

Bit by bit, with everyone taking part, the whole story came out.

Mama was horrified. "How could you do such a thing?" she scolded. "What happened to your manners? How could you sit down and eat with nobody there?"

"But, Mama, it said in the note we should," Charlotte pleaded.

Mama turned to the woman. "I must apologize for my children. Usually they have better manners. They never did anything like this before, I promise you."

The woman waved it away. "Don't take it to heart. So they ate a supper in my house. What's wrong with that? Believe me, I enjoyed seeing so many nice young faces around my table."

"It was very wrong of them." Mama frowned. "They had no right. . . ."

Lena wouldn't let her finish. She placed a plump arm on Mama's. "Oh, you children! You ate up the lady's supper! They ate up the whole supper! Don't

you see how funny it is? Oh! Oh! Oh!" She threw back her head and shrieked with laughter. Soon everyone was laughing, and no one was laughing harder than the woman herself.

"Next—time—" she wheezed between gasps, "next time—children—let me know—when you're coming—so I'll cook enough."

"Well, neighbor," Lena said, wiping her eyes, "what is your name?"

"It's Mrs. Shiner—Molly Shiner."

"This certainly was a comical way for us to meet, Mrs. Shiner. Listen, please. I've got plenty of food downstairs. There is enough for twenty people! Leave another note on the table for your husband and your son and come downstairs with us. Everybody is invited for supper!"

Focus

1. At the start of the story, what were the children trying to find?
2. The children went to the wrong apartment. What mistake did they make that let them do that?
3. How did the children feel when they found out their mistake?
4. Lena and Mrs. Shiner both thought it was funny. What did Lena do to help make up for the mistake?

Teresa tries to help her family. Then she has to help get herself out of trouble!

THE ENDLESS HALLWAYS OF THE AIRPORT

R. CONRAD STEIN

Teresa stood in line at the Los Angeles airport. In a short time she would be in the city of Mérida, in Mexico. Her family was on its way to see her grandmother.

"What's on your mind?" Teresa's mother asked.

"*Pozole*," said Teresa, rubbing her tummy.

Her mother smiled. "All you think about is food!"

"But I can't help it. Grandma's *pozole* is so good! You know how she has those big chunks of pork and corn in that good stew gravy! And that yummy chicken with the good sauce she makes—remember how good that tastes?"

Teresa stopped short and thought a minute. "Mom, what did Grandma call the custard she made?"

"Do you mean *flan*?" asked her mother. "Oh— here comes your father. If we want some of that good

23

food, we've got to find out where we get on the plane."

"OK! I got the bags checked in," said Teresa's father. "Let's get ourselves on that plane. It leaves from Gate 41." He started to walk down the hall.

Teresa almost had to run to keep up. There were crowds of people going up and down the long hallways. Teresa looked up at her baby brother. He rested in her mother's arms. He's too little to care about the trip to Mexico, thought Teresa.

As they walked, Teresa's father bent down. He took her hand. "We'll arrive at Grandma's in time for supper. Tonight I'll take you out. We'll see the little bands that play music in the street. They're called *mariachis*, and they play lively music."

"That sounds like fun," said Teresa. "I can't wait to hear them!"

Her father smiled as they hurried down the hallway.

Teresa looked up at her brother again. That Billy! He got his hands into everything! He was digging in her mother's purse. Billy pulled the keys out. He loved to play with keys. Teresa's mother didn't see what Billy was up to.

"This way," said Teresa's father. He went to the escalator that was moving up.

The escalator had risen only a few steps when Billy threw the keys over the side. They fell to the floor below.

"Mother! Look what Billy did!" said Teresa.

"Flight 710 from Dallas is now arriving at Gate 47." The deep voice on the loudspeaker drowned out Teresa's words. Her mother had not heard her.

"Mother! Billy dropped your keys!"

"Passengers on Flight 54 to Tokyo, please board your plane." Again the loudspeaker drowned out Teresa.

"I'll go get the keys myself," she thought. "I'll only be a minute."

Teresa turned around. She tried to walk down the escalator. She walked and walked. It seemed as if she were just standing still. Then she ran down the moving steps. It took a minute, but she finally reached the bottom.

Teresa found the keys on the floor. The key-ring held the car keys and the house keys. Her mother would be pleased Teresa had found them.

Teresa put the keys in her pocket and ran back up the escalator.

At the top she found hallways leading left and right. There were crowds of people rushing back and forth.

"Mom? Dad?" Teresa called.

There was no answer.

Teresa's eyes darted left and right. She could not

see her parents. "Oh, boy," she said to herself. "I guess I'm lost in this big old airport! I've got to find Mom and Dad somehow. I'll just start walking."

There were hundreds of people around, but Teresa felt very, very frightened.

"But which way should I go?" thought Teresa. "Should I go to the left or should I go to the right?"

All at once she remembered what her father had said. Their plane was leaving from Gate 41. She looked at the hallway on her right. There she saw a sign that said Gate 45. Then she looked at the hallway on her left. That sign said Gate 44. A sign farther down the hall said Gate 43.

"I'd better go to the left," Teresa said in a whisper.

Teresa walked past Gate 44 and Gate 43. She was going the right way, but where were her parents? How could they have gotten so far ahead of her?

At Gate 42 she started to run. There were so many people, she couldn't see very far. Were they here? Twice she almost spoke to someone, only to find out it was a stranger. Where were they? Would they get on

the plane without her? Finally, she found them! "Momma! Dad!" she called.

"Teresa! Where have you been?" asked her mother. She hugged Teresa with one arm.

"I was just going to go back and look for you," said her father.

"I knew I had to go to Gate 41. So I followed the signs," Teresa said.

"That's what I was hoping you'd do," her father said. "I'm glad I have such a smart daughter."

Teresa's mother looked at her sternly. "How did you get away from us in the first place?"

"Because of these." Teresa pulled the keys out of her pocket. "Billy picked them out of your purse and threw them over the side of the escalator. I went to get them."

Quickly Teresa's mother looked in her purse. "Those are my keys. I didn't know they were gone! Oh, thank goodness you found them."

"Good work!" said Teresa's father. "Well, let's go! We've got to get on that plane if we want to get to Mexico."

Focus

1. Where were Teresa and her family going?
2. What made Teresa walk back down the escalator?
3. What did Teresa remember that helped her find her family?
4. Teresa's father was proud of her quick thinking. What did he say that showed he was proud?
5. Do you think Teresa did the right thing to go get the keys? Could she have thought of a better way to handle the problem?

Here are some photographs of the Los Angeles airport.

PICTURES AT THE AIRPORT

DEVRA LIEB

Airline passengers are always in a hurry. They run with their bags. They wave tickets in the air. They make arrangements to meet people. They look out the big glass windows to find their planes.

But not long ago, at the Los Angeles Airport, something made the busy passengers stop. They saw something on the walls. And they smiled. They saw murals of the airport. One picture showed a big red plane and a bright yellow van. In another picture, there was a yellow tower. There was a family holding hands so that no one would get lost. And biggest of all was the airport restaurant, looking like a big mushroom

31

with wings.

These murals were special ones. They were made by students from schools in Los Angeles. Their teachers had brought them to the airport. Tour guides showed the classes the waiting rooms. The students went all over the airport. They met some of the workers. Finally, it was time to leave. The tour guides asked if the classes would like to draw what they had seen.

Back at school, the children got to work. They remembered the friendliness of their guides, so they worked hard. They drew planes. They drew people. They cut out buildings. Finally they put it all together.

Their murals were done. They sent the pictures to the airport.

The airport workers hung the murals on the walls. The passengers going by stopped. And they smiled. For a long time they would remember the pictures at the airport.

Focus

1. Who made the murals?
2. Name three things that the students saw at the airport.
3. Tell how the students made the murals.

33

LIFE SKILL: Emergency Directions

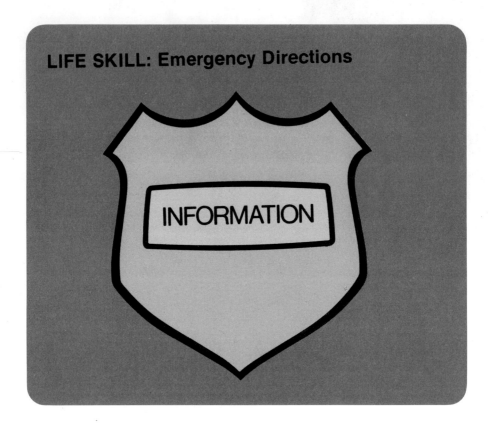

Teresa got lost in the airport. She found her parents by careful thinking. Would you know what to do if you were lost in a public place? Here are some things to keep in mind.

Try to stay calm. Stop and look around. Do you know where you are supposed to be? If so, look for signs to show you how to get there.

It may be that you don't know where you should go. In that case, look for a booth marked "Information" or "Courtesy." The workers in such a booth may wear uniforms or badges. Part of their job is to help people with problems. They can help you with yours.

Getting lost is not as scary as you think if you know what to do. Keep these things in mind.

IF YOU GET LOST

Try to stay calm.
Look for signs to help you.
Look for an information or courtesy booth.
Ask a person wearing a uniform or badge for help.

Now see if you can answer these questions. Write your answers on a sheet of paper.

1. How can signs help you?
2. What are the names of the booths you should look for?
3. Name one way to know who can help you.

Workers in a public place are paid to help other people.
Sometimes people volunteer to help others.

THE
VOLUNTEER
FIRE TEAM

ROSEMARY M. LAWSON

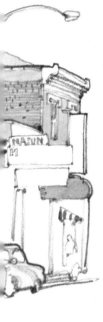

It is Tuesday morning. Everyone in the small town is busy at work.

At 10:22 A.M. there is one blast on the noisy horn. The druggist stops filling the bottle on her counter. The garage man leaves a car up on the lift. The butcher takes off his apron. The barber leaves her shop. Women who work at home scoop up their children and run for their cars.

No one is surprised that all these people quit work. Others fill in for them at their jobs. The horn is the signal for the Volunteer Fire Team to come put out a fire. Only the Volunteer Fire Team will go to the fire.

Some members of the team go right to the firehouse. They will drive the trucks to the fire. They work nearby, so they can get there quickly. Other team members will go right to the fire. They have two-way radios in their cars. They find out where the fire is while they drive.

This fire is on the north side of town, on Frederick Street. The Lugos' big farm is there. Their house or barns may be in danger.

At 10:24 A.M. Peg Smith gets to the firehouse. She is a barber who works two doors down from the

firehouse. She jumps into the pumper and starts the engine.

It is 10:26 A.M. Peg pulls her truck out of the firehouse. Luis Borjas, the butcher, jumps in next to her. Their fire gear is already on the truck. Luis will put on his big boots and heavy coat on the way to the fire. The team members have practiced many times. Each one knows just when to do every part of the job.

Gina Ortero and Bill Adams run to the Rescue Unit truck. Bill starts the engine just as Craig Scott gets in the back.

Gina is a druggist in town. As part of her work, she knows a lot about health. But to be on the Rescue Unit, Gina, Bill, and Craig had to take extra training.

Chris Sousa climbs in the back of the hook-and-ladder truck. Clay Jones starts the engine.

The hook-and-ladder truck needs two drivers. It is so long that it has an extra steering wheel at the back. Chris is called the "tiller driver." He rides in a special

cab high above the rest of the truck. He steers the back wheels when the truck goes around corners. That is a special job to learn. The back wheels must be turned the opposite way from the front wheels.

At 10:27 A.M. the hook-and-ladder truck clears the firehouse doors. Bob Jaffee shuts the garage-type doors. He goes back to his desk. Five minutes ago Bob blew the fire horn. All the trucks have gone out now, but Bob's job is not over.

One member of the team always stays at the firehouse to answer the phone. There could be another fire in town at the same time. Or, if the fire is a big one, the team may need more help. Then someone at the fire will call back to the firehouse. Bob will phone the next town. That town will send its volunteers to the fire.

At 10:34 A.M. Mary Secrist and Marge Hews reach the fire. First they dropped their children off at a friend's house. Now they have driven to the fire. Mary parks her car and pulls on her boots and coat. They run to check on the Lugos' safety. A field is burning, close to the barn, but nobody is in danger. Mary and Marge get the area ready. Marge makes sure there will be space for the fire trucks to park. Mary checks to see how many hoses will be needed to get the water to the fire.

It is 10:36 A.M. Other members of the fire team drive up. They have left their homes and jobs. Now they get ready to fight the fire.

At 10:37 A.M. the trucks pull up to the fire. One group gets the pumper ready. Other people pull out the hoses.

Gina and Craig go to the barn. The barn is not burning, but they move the animals to a safe place. If the smoke reaches the barn, it will frighten the animals. Frightened animals could get in the way and slow down the fire team.

It is 10:48 A.M. Tom Sainz is the Fire Chief. He has

41

a plan to fight this blaze. He tells the team to pump 25 gallons a minute onto the fire. The team works hard and fast. Another hose wets down the area where the fire is heading. It works! The fire makes a lot of smoke, but the fire fighters keep it from reaching the barn.

It is 11:17 A.M. The fire is getting smaller. Soon it will be out. The long ladder from the hook-and-ladder was not needed. Chris and Clay have been doing other jobs. Chief Sainz tells them that the fire is under control. They can go back to the station.

By 11:32 A.M. the smoke has died down. Chief Sainz checks the area carefully. The team pours water on it until the Chief is sure it won't flare up again.

At 11:57 A.M. Chief Sainz decides that the fire is out. Luis calls the fire station. The trucks will go back to the firehouse soon.

It is 11:58 A.M. Back at the station, Bob gives two short blasts on the fire horn. All over town, people know that the fire is out. The members of the team will go back to their other jobs soon.

As the trucks come back to the station, there is more work to do. The fire station is a busy place for a while. A report must be written about what happened at the fire. Each piece of equipment has to be put back where it belongs. It must be ready for the next fire.

It is 12:43 P.M. The pumper gets back to the

firehouse. It is the last truck to come in. Its hoses have to be dried, so that they won't rot. One by one the firefighters turn back into druggists, barbers, and store clerks.

The people on the Volunteer Fire Team feel good about the job they have done. The Lugos' farm is safe and no one was hurt.

Everyone on the fire team lives and works in the small town. There are not enough fires in the town to have a full-time fire department. Instead, people give up their free time. They learn how to fight fires quickly and safely. They learn how to care for the equipment, too.

The volunteer firefighters work well together. They know that their own houses and the places where they work are safe. The town has a good team to protect it from fires.

Focus

1. How do the volunteers know they are needed to fight a fire?
2. Why does one person always stay at the fire station?
3. What signal is given in this town when the fire has been put out?
4. Why do some towns have a volunteer fire team instead of a paid fire department?

CHECKPOINT

Vocabulary: Word Identification

Find the best word for each sentence. Write your own sentences for the words that are left over.

suggested   students   volunteer

Mexico   enjoyed   garage

1. "Why don't you write your letter later?" _____ Anna.
2. Who will _____ to water the plants?
3. Mark _____ himself at the party.

Comprehension: Referents

Read the sentences about Jake Smith. Find the word that is underlined. Then answer the questions on your paper.

Jake Smith's family moved to the city, where they live in a tall building. It is much bigger than the Smith's old home.

4. What does the word *it* stand for?

the Smith's old home   the city   a tall building

Soon Jake meets a boy named Stan. He and Jake have the same guitar teacher.

5. What does the word *he* stand for?

Jake   Stan   the guitar teacher

Jake and Stan have a good time playing songs at their guitar lessons. They have become good friends.

6. What does the word *they* stand for?

guitar lessons   songs   Jake and Stan

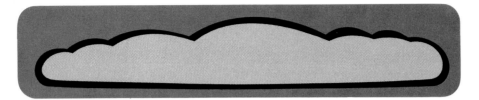

Pick the right word from the list to complete each sentence. Write the sentences on your paper.

Decoding:
Inflection
(*f* to *ve* before *-s*)

life—lives   loaf—loaves   half—halves

7. Do cats have nine _____ ?

8. Mom asked Sam to buy a _____ of bread.

9. Two _____ make a whole.

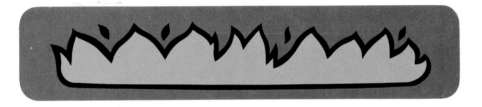

Read the Emergency Directions below. Then answer the questions that follow. Write the answers on your paper.

Life Skills:
Directions
(emergency)

IN CASE OF FIRE
A. Stay calm.
B. Walk to the nearest exit. Do not run.
C. Leave the building.
D. Move away from the building.

10. What is the first thing to remember?

11. What exit should you go to?

12. What do you do after you leave the building?

the silent cat
at the tenement
window, sniffs
the noises and
alarms—stares
out the window
expressionless,
his tail anchored
to another sound.

DAVID KHERDIAN

47

Helping others makes the helper feel good.
Ah Jim finds there can be other rewards, too.

The Rice Bowl Pet

PATRICIA MILES MARTIN

Ah Jim lived in Chinatown.

From the window of his apartment he could see balconies and roof tops. Over the roof tops the sea gulls swooped high in the sky above San Francisco Bay.

On the balconies of the houses, his neighbors watered their plants and played with their pets. There was a woman with a red and gold parrot in a cage, and a man with a black cat on his shoulder. Ah Jim liked to watch the parrot and the cat.

He said to his mother one day, "I would like to have a pet." His mother was busy cooking. She didn't even look at him.

He said it three times before his mother answered. "Our family is big and our apartment is small," she

said. "There is not much room. But you may have a small pet. It must be little enough to fit in a rice bowl."

At supper, when Ah Jim ate his rice, he held his chopsticks carefully and did not spill a single grain. He looked at his rice bowl. It was very small.

"I don't know what pet I want," he said.

His brothers laughed at him.

"Do you want a turtle?" they asked. "Do you want a cricket?"

But Ah Jim didn't know.

The next morning Ah Jim went to school. He was polite to everyone. He said his lessons for the teacher.

At noon he ate his lunch in the big schoolyard with his friends.

"Have you a pet?" he asked Linda.

"I have a little turtle," said his friend.

"I have a cricket," said Ping Loo.

A turtle or a cricket would be small enough to fit in

a rice bowl. But Ah Jim would have to keep the turtle in a glass jar, and the cricket in a bamboo cage. The turtle would not be free to crawl and the cricket would not be free to jump.

He knew that he didn't want a turtle or a cricket.

After school, Ah Jim went down the street to a Chinese language school. He learned about the watch towers on the Great Wall of China. He learned about sampans on the Yellow River. He learned to read and write in Cantonese.

When Saturday came, he looked at his rice bowl again. "I'll take it with me," he said, "and find a pet that will fit." He walked up the hill to the shops. Every shop had things to look at. In one window he saw a tiny jade elephant.

"There is a pet that would go in my rice bowl," he said. But he did not want a jade elephant. He wanted a live pet.

51

Through the window, he saw something run across the shop. It was a little dog, the littlest dog he had ever seen. It was the color of gold, with two eyes and a nose like three shining black buttons. It jumped into a small basket.

The dog would make a nice pet. It was almost what he wanted, but not quite.

It would not fit in the rice bowl.

As Ah Jim looked through the shop window, the glass felt cold and smooth against his nose. Two black-button eyes looked back at him from over the side of the basket.

The shopkeeper came outside.

"Do not press your face against my window," he said. "Boys and girls come to look at the dogs in my shop, and I must always wash this window after they leave."

Ah Jim hurried away, carrying his empty bowl carefully.

After his lunch, Ah Jim went out to play. He still carried his rice bowl.

He thought about the golden dog he had seen in the store. If only it were small enough to fit in his rice bowl!

"Why don't you go to a pet shop?" asked his brother. "Maybe you'll see something little."

As Ah Jim was walking toward the pet shop, he met a boy from his school.

"What are you carrying?" asked Ah Jim.

"A frog," the boy said.

"Can I hold it?" Ah Jim asked.

The boy held Ah Jim's bowl, and Ah Jim held the frog. One minute the frog was in his hands, and the next minute it was gone.

It had hopped inside his shirt.

Ah Jim hopped too, while he reached for the frog.

I do not want a frog, he thought. It is too cold. I want a warm pet.

At the pet shop, he saw many animals: a big monkey swinging on a bar, a green parrot on a perch, a black cat with a silver bell around its neck. Then he saw two parakeets. They were small. Just the right size to go in a rice bowl.

Ah Jim looked at them. He did not want two parakeets. He wanted a pet he could hold.

On the way home, he thought of little things: worms, guppies, snails. . . .

He decided to go to Fisherman's Wharf.

He climbed aboard a cable car and sat outside. On the turns, the gripman called in a loud voice: "Watch out for the curve!"

Ah Jim slid along the wooden seat and held tightly

to his rice bowl. At the end of the line was Fisherman's Wharf. He wandered around and looked at the fishing boats rocking in the water.

He smelled the seafood cooking in the brick vats along the walk. He looked for a pet.

A crab is too large, he thought. A lobster is too large. And even if they were small, they are not good pets, for they nip a finger unless you are careful.

He decided he did not want a crab or a lobster.

He wanted a pet he could hold, a pet that was warm, a pet that would fit in his rice bowl.

He could not forget the dog that was the color of gold, the dog that was almost little enough to fit in his rice bowl.

He rode back to Chinatown, and when at last he reached the shop with the jade elephant in the window, he stopped. The little dog was still there. Ah Jim pushed his face against the windowpane.

The shopkeeper came outside.

"You again," he said. He shook his head sadly. "You come to look through my window, and so I do nothing but wash off finger and face marks all day long. Please go."

Ah Jim saw that the windowpane was covered with smudges. He turned and ran.

Around the corner, he stopped. He thought about all the fingermarks on the windowpane, the smudges he had made. He went back to the shop.

The shopkeeper was starting to wash the window and he scowled when he saw Ah Jim.

Ah Jim spoke quickly. "I would like to wash the window for you."

"But the marks here are not all your fingermarks," the shopkeeper said.

"I know," said Ah Jim, "but many are mine. I will wash the window."

"Very good," said the shopkeeper.

Ah Jim set his rice bowl down on the walk and started to work.

He cleaned and polished, watching the golden dog all the while. Then he cleaned and polished again. There was not a single mark left.

When the window was shining bright, he looked inside and saw the shopkeeper and his wife laughing there.

"Come in, come in," the shopkeeper called. "My wife and I have thought of a very good thing."

Ah Jim went inside.

"Tomorrow," the shopkeeper said, "the little dog goes back to China with our brother. Our brother leaves one puppy." He reached inside the small basket.

There in the shopkeeper's hand was the tiniest puppy Ah Jim had ever seen. The man handed it to him.

"Now," said the shopkeeper, "if you will take this puppy, there will be no reason for boys and girls to come to our window to press noses and hands against our clean glass, for the dogs will be gone."

The puppy was the color of gold.

It was warm.

And it was just the right size to fit into his rice bowl.

Ah Jim tried to thank the man, but no words came.

The woman smiled. "Do not speak," she said. "We see your thanks in your face."

Ah Jim walked down the street, carefully carrying the puppy in his rice bowl. Its bark, he knew, would be

no louder than the sound of bamboo wind chimes hanging in a doorway.

He walked down the hill and up the stairs to his apartment.

"Look," he said. "It fits in my rice bowl."

His brothers laughed, and after a while, his mother laughed too.

Ah Jim laughed the longest of all.

Focus

1. Ah Jim's mother said he could have a pet, but the pet would have to fit into a rice bowl. Why did she say that?

2. Ah Jim saw many kinds of pets. One was a parakeet. Name two other pets he saw. Tell why he did not want them for his pet.

3. What kind of pet did Ah Jim find? Tell how he found his pet.

MATH READING: What's It All About?

Ah Jim wanted a pet to fit his rice bowl. There are many ways to measure things. You can learn about measuring in a math book. Here are some tips to help you do your math reading.

TAKE A FIRST LOOK

Look at the math page and find the title and two headings. What will you do in the first set of exercises?

The smaller headings under the main headings are called *subheadings.* These subheadings tell you what to do.

Notice the pictures on the page. They will show you what is being measured.

FIND THE KEY IDEAS

Read the subheadings. The first one tells you to add. What does the second subheading tell you to do?

Look at the word problems. How will the labels below the pictures help you do these problems?

READ CAREFULLY

What is the number of the last exercise you add? What is the number of the first exercise you subtract?

When you copy the exercises onto your paper, be sure to number them. Check what you write.

Read word problems slowly. Be sure you know what to do. Use the labels for the pictures to solve the problems.

MEASURE UP

Number Exercises
Add

1. 46
     +23

2. 45
     +32

3. 267
     + 31

4. 684
     +815

5. 548
     +836

6. 10+97=_____

7. 11+19=_____

8. 12+79=_____

Subtract

9. 79
     −64

10. 87
      −68

11. 78
      −59

12. 49
      −40

13. 88
      −59

Word Problems

21 inches
53 cm

18 inches
46 cm

6 inches
15 cm

The art class has been making clay animals. They want to have a show.

14. What is the length of the dog and the cat together?

15. How much longer than the bird is the cat?

16. Which is the longest animal?

61

Ah Jim's pet was the answer to his problem. Jessica's pet, Boots, was the cause of her problem.

Applesauce

SUZANNE HIGGINS

"A friend in need is a friend indeed. And Sue, this friend sure is in need." Jessica sounded unhappy as she spoke on the telephone. "Can you please come to my house and help me decide what to do?"

Sue agreed, and Jessica felt better already. It was good to know that Sue would help out. Jessica petted her cat, Boots. The big tabby purred as it climbed into Jessica's lap.

"You're a good cat, Boots, but you're the one who caused all this trouble."

Just then Jessica heard her mother call.

"Lunch is ready. Come and eat your omelet before it gets cold."

Jessica's tummy growled. She sure was hungry. Boots was asleep, and Jessica hated to wake her up. Favorite cat or not, Jessica decided her omelet was more important than a cat's nap. She lifted Boots gently from her lap and put her on a pillow. "Don't worry, Boots," she whispered. "Sue and I'll work something out."

As she walked into the kitchen, her mother said, "Eat your omelet, Jessica, and then sweep the front porch. I'm going to a meeting about the Town Fair. I'll be next door at Ms. Mayer's until two o'clock."

The Town Fair was the best event of the summer. Jessica was usually very excited about it. But before she could even start thinking about the fair, she had something else to do. She reached for a box beneath the table. Inside were three playful, blond kittens.

"What am I going to do with all of you?" she asked the furry little balls. She was beginning to love these kittens already, but she knew she couldn't keep them. Her family rented their house from people who didn't allow pets. As a special favor, Jessica had been allowed to keep Boots. Three more cats were out of the question.

Sadly Jessica sat at the table and began to eat. All through lunch she thought about what to do. When she had eaten almost all of her omelet, she went outside to sweep. She pushed the dust around a bit and thought about her problem. The more she thought about it, the more horrible it seemed. By the time Sue arrived, Jessica was just standing and thinking and not sweeping at all.

"Hi!" Sue said. "Finish your sweeping and let's go inside. I've got the answer to part of your problem."

In no time the porch was clean, and the girls were sitting in the kitchen. With a wide grin, Sue pulled a box from behind her back. Jessica opened it and saw a soft towel tucked inside.

"Oh, Sue! Does this mean your mom will let you keep one of the kittens?" asked Jessica.

"That's right," said Sue, "and I know just the one I want. I want the one with the hazel eyes. It looks just like Boots!"

67

"That's wonderful," cried Jessica. "This little kitten has the best luck. It will be living with you."

"Now you have to do me a favor," said Sue. "My mother wants me to pick up a package at Mrs. Johnson's house. You can come with me."

"Ugh!" complained Jessica. "I don't want to go there! Mrs. Johnson always talks about eating right and staying healthy!"

"I know. Isn't it awful?" said Sue. "But she does make the best applesauce in town. I'm supposed to pick some up for dessert tonight."

"Well, I guess it's the least I can do," said Jessica. "After all, you did solve one of my problems."

As they walked to Mrs. Johnson's house, Sue spoke with excitement about her plans for her new pet. "I think I'll call her Gabrielle. That's my favorite name. Do you think she'll be big enough to be in the Pet Show?"

The Pet Show! Jessica had been planning on putting Boots in the Town Fair Pet Show, but now she wouldn't be able to. It took time to get Boots ready. All her time would be spent trying to find homes for the other kittens.

Just then, the two girls realized that they had already reached Mrs. Johnson's house.

"I'll wait here for you, Sue," said Jessica.

"Oh, no," said Sue, "you're coming with me. I'll just give her this note my mom wrote. We won't have to stay very long."

The girls knocked on the door. After a while Mrs. Johnson answered. She opened the door, saying, "Sue! Jessica! I'm working in my vegetable garden, but I'll be through in a minute. Please come in."

Sue quickly handed Mrs. Johnson the note.

"Applesauce!" said Mrs. Johnson. "Well, you are here on the right day. I always make applesauce on Thursday. You girls can come and wait in the kitchen. I'll get my vegetables from the garden and then put some fresh applesauce in jars for your family's dessert."

Jessica and Sue followed Mrs. Johnson to the kitchen and sat down at the table. Before they could say a word, Mrs. Johnson gave them each an extra-big slice of bread and a huge bowl of applesauce.

"There is nothing healthier than girls who eat applesauce. If you want to be healthy, you'll eat every last drop," said Mrs. Johnson. Jessica and Sue looked at each other. Sue bit her lip to keep from giggling. "Thank you," she called as Mrs. Johnson hurried out the door.

Soon Mrs. Johnson returned with two jars of applesauce and a smile. "Good heavens! You look healthier already!" she said as she sat down.

"You know, it's nice having company . . . it's not the same living here anymore. It gets too lonely. I used to have a big tabby cat. She's gone now, and I miss her very much. She was certainly good company for me. Why, she even liked the same television shows that I did! Now that she's gone, I don't even like to watch television. It makes me miss her even more."

As Jessica listened, she realized that Mrs. Johnson was lonely. Jessica thought for a moment. Suddenly she had an idea.

"Thank you for the dessert," said Jessica. "We have to leave now. If you don't mind, I'd like to come back soon and visit you."

"Of course. Come back any time. I love having your company," said Mrs. Johnson.

As they walked out the door, Sue said, "What were you talking about? I thought you didn't like Mrs. Johnson."

"She's really very kind," said Jessica, "even if she does talk about being healthy. She needs company. And the truth is, we need Mrs. Johnson!"

Sue knew her friend was up to something, but she didn't understand exactly what. The two friends walked back to Jessica's house in silence. As soon as they got to her house, Jessica went to find her mom, and Sue went to play with the kittens. A few minutes later Jessica came into the kitchen looking for a basket. She found one just the right size. She also found a towel that fit into it. Sue watched Jessica reach beneath the table and get two sleeping kittens from the box. Now Sue began to understand her friend's plan.

"Jessica! That's a wonderful idea! Mrs. Johnson will love having kittens again!"

Jessica knew that her idea was a good one. She was sad that the kittens were leaving her. But she knew she would be able to see all three of them grow up.

"Let's go, Sue," said Jessica. "Mrs. Johnson is going to see us sooner than she thinks!" The two girls hurried all the way to Mrs. Johnson's house and rang the bell.

Mrs. Johnson answered her door quickly this time. Jessica smiled as she handed her the basket.

"Mrs. Johnson," Jessica said, "I want very much for you to have these kittens. They need someone to take

care of them. I know you will give them a very good home. I even named them for you. This one is Apple, and this one is Sauce."

"Oh my, how wonderful!" cried Mrs. Johnson. "They're certainly the most beautiful kittens I've ever seen. And what perfect names you've given them." Mrs. Johnson gave each of the girls a hug and thanked them again.

"We have to go now," said Jessica. "Sue and I have to start getting our own pets ready for the Pet Show at the Town Fair."

"I have an idea!" said Sue. "Mrs. Johnson, you're such a good cook! Why don't you enter your applesauce in the Town Fair? I'm sure you would win a blue ribbon."

"Why thank you, Sue," said Mrs. Johnson, "but it looks like I'm going to have my fill of Apple and Sauce right here in my own home!"

Focus

1. What was Jessica worried about at the beginning of the story?
2. How did Sue help Jessica?
3. What idea did Jessica have at Mrs. Johnson's house?
4. Tell how Jessica was a good friend to Sue and to Mrs. Johnson.

Just like Sue and Jessica, Eric and Jon are best friends. On this summer day, they are waiting for something special.

A Summer Day with ERIC

BARBARA KAFFEE ATKINS

Eric lives in a yellow two-family house with brown shutters on a dead end street. He knows his house is yellow with brown shutters because his best friend Jon told him. Eric has been blind since he was five.

In this yellow house with brown shutters, Eric and his family live downstairs. Jon and his family live upstairs. Jon's room is right above Eric's room. Eric and Jon share a secret code.

Every summer morning Eric taps on the heating pipe to tell Jon that he will meet him in fifteen minutes. Three short taps means they are going fishing this morning. Jon hurries to get dressed, eating his oatmeal quickly. Eric puts new hooks and sinkers in his tackle

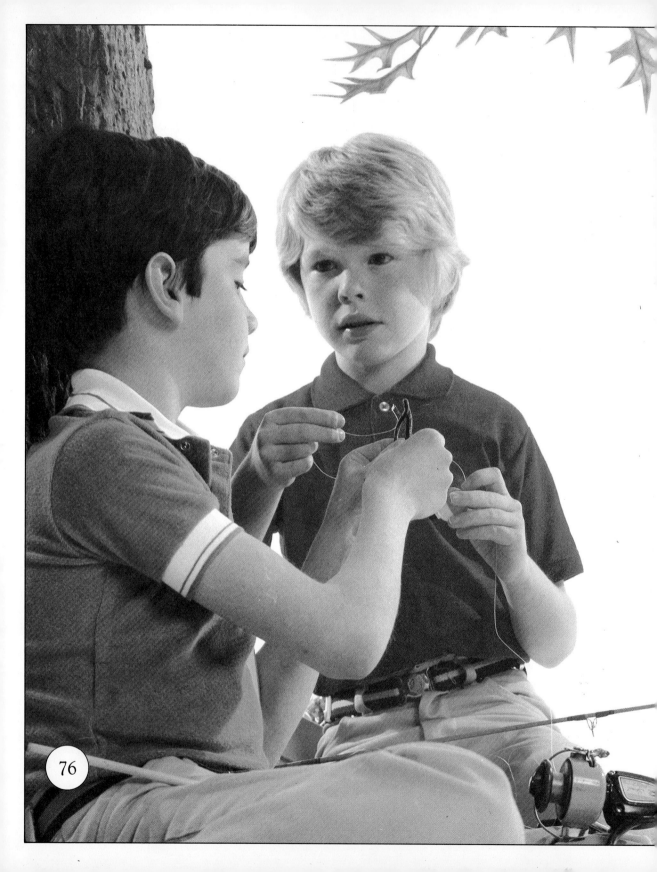

box. They meet in the hall.

"I can't believe this is it! Today's the day our special wheels will arrive!" Jon exclaims. They walk to the lake through the apple orchard. They stop at a tree where the apples are ripe and heavy on the limbs.

Eric smiles and his toes wiggle inside his damp sneakers.

"I'm glad we saved our newspaper route money for one whole year to buy special wheels," Eric says. He leans against the tree, feeling the warm sun on his face. A fuzzy creature crawls up his arm. He cups it in his hand. "Jon, what's this?"

"It's a striped caterpillar!" Jon says. Eric gives the caterpillar to his friend. He picks a couple of fist-sized apples from the tree.

At the lake they unpack their fishing gear. Eric takes two wiggly worms from the box. "Here's your worm," he says. "Let's cast our lines together. One, two, three, cast your line!" There is a splash as both lines hit the water.

They wait for the fish to bite. "That sun is getting hot. It's a good thing there's a breeze," Eric says.

Jon describes the morning sky to his friend. "The water is rippled and the whole lake sparkles. The sky is very blue with stacks of fluffy clouds."

"Wait!" Eric says. "Listen carefully! Can you hear

that hummingbird? When we ride our special wheels, we'll sound like a whole flock of hummingbirds!"

They talk about the special wheels they ordered and about the fish they caught last summer. They tell each other riddles. Eric asks Jon a new riddle.

"If two is a couple and three is a crowd, what are four and five?"

Jon thinks and then gives up.

"The answer is nine!" Eric says, and they both laugh.

Suddenly there is a tug on Eric's fishing line. He reels it up.

"It's a beauty! A blue and yellow sunfish!" Jon shouts.

Eric takes the fish off the hook, and hands it to Jon. Jon puts it on the stringer. "Eric, you always catch the first fish," Jon says.

After Jon reels in a catfish, they set their fishing poles on the grass and unpack their lunches. "The smell of those peanut butter sandwiches makes me hungry," says Eric. "Oh! The first swallow of lemonade made my tongue curl!" He shares half of his carrot cake with Jon before they pack up their gear.

On their way home they go to the park and ride on the seesaw. "Jon, I feel like a balloon that's been let go! Close your eyes—do you feel that way, too?" Eric asks.

"Oh, that's neat! When I go up quickly—yipes! My balloon burst when you bumped down hard!"

They go into the open field to play leap frog. When they stop, Jon says, "Eric, count for me while I stand on my head. OK, I'm ready! Count!"

"One, two, three. . . ." Eric counts quickly, then slows down and speeds up again. Jon tumbles down, laughing.

"My turn," says Eric. "You watch and count for me." Eric becomes a human snowball. He does five somersaults without stopping.

"Do you think our wheels have been delivered yet?" Eric asks.

"I hope so," Jon answers. "Let's go home and find out." When they arrive home, they rush into the garage.

"They're not here yet," Jon says.

"Sh . . . ," Eric warns him. "I hear a scratching noise."

They listen and search between the workbench and the water bucket. "There it is! It's a little tan kitten!" Jon shouts. "It must have wandered over from next door. There was a sign on the porch that said *Free Kittens.*"

Eric holds the kitten against his face. "You're a soft

surprise," he says as he pets the kitten's fur. "Hey! Why is your nose so wet?"

"It was covered with soap bubbles from the bucket," says Jon.

"Let's call him Suds!" says Eric. "And let's go ask Mom if I can keep him."

Eric's mother is in the front room. Suds has just calmed down on Eric's lap when there is a loud toot out front. "Yipes! Those claws are sharp! Here, Mom, you hold Suds," says Eric.

"It's the delivery truck! Our wheels are here!" Jon says as they hurry outdoors again. "Eric, we can really move on this beauty! We can get our newspaper route done in no time." They reach the bike and he guides Eric's hands to it.

"Here's the pedal, just like on the trike I used to have," Eric says. "It won't be too hard to learn to ride this thing! As soon as we do, let's give Suds a ride on our bicycle-built-for-two!"

Focus

1. How did Eric and Jon send messages to each other?
2. Describe what Eric and Jon did in the park.
3. What did they want to use the special wheels for?
4. What was the special thing Eric and Jon were waiting for?

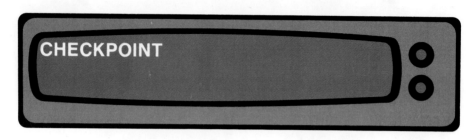

CHECKPOINT

Read the questions below. Write each correct answer on your paper.

1. Which word means "something you like the best"?
   flavor   favorite   fable   most
2. Which word means "something you can watch"?
   terrible   air   ideas   television
3. Which word means "to tell about something"?
   describe   follow   imagine   words
4. Which word means "only one"?
   swing   single   two   song
5. Which word means "to take things out of a box or bag"?
   under   undress   unpack   unlock

Read the sentences below. On your paper, write the sentence that tells what the underlined words mean.

6. The plane's roar <u>split the air</u>.
   a. The plane cut the air.
   b. The plane made a loud sound.
   c. The plane was in the air.

7. A <u>wave of fear</u> passed over Chris.

    a. Chris went swimming.

    b. Chris waved at fear.

    c. Chris was afraid.

8. The <u>light dawned</u> on the girls.

    a. The girls understood.

    b. The sun rose.

    c. The girls turned down the light.

Read each sentence below. Choose the correct word to complete each sentence. Write the words on your paper.

Decoding:
Vowels
ou(gh)
au(gh)

9. When I was sick, I had to _____.

    numb   cough   walk

10. She _____ the runner at home base.

    combed   tough   caught

11. A sunflower grows on a tall_____.

    ghost   stalk   tough

Using Our Sen

Two of the senses are sight and hearing. Smell, touch, and taste are the other senses. People and animals need these senses to live. Some animals can use their senses better than humans can. But animals don't have some things people have. One is a "sense of humor." Another is a "sense of beauty."

These next stories tell about how the world works. Some of the stories are funny. Some may be a little scary. Some are make-believe. Read the stories to find out about using senses.

ses

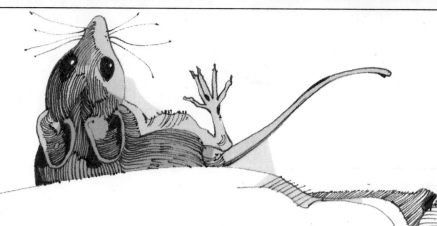

Some animals are large. Others are small. Sometimes it's good to be small, like the bear mouse.

Bear Mouse in Winter

BERNIECE FRESCHET

The sun was low in the sky. The bear mouse would have to return to her babies soon. But first she needed more to eat. She had to find food to make milk for her young, or they would starve.

Overhead the cardinal flashed by. Something dropped from his bill. A red holly berry lay in the snow.

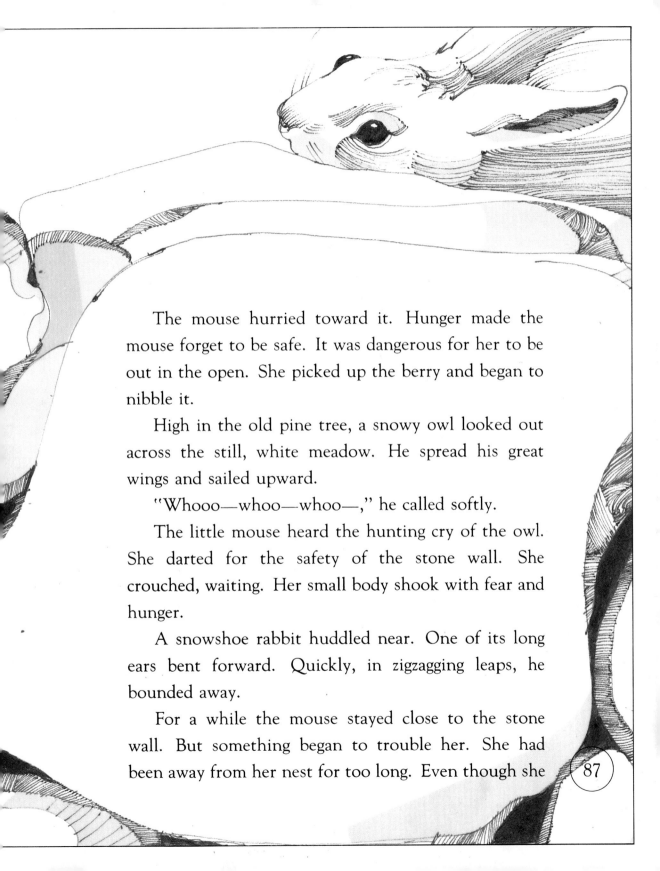

The mouse hurried toward it. Hunger made the mouse forget to be safe. It was dangerous for her to be out in the open. She picked up the berry and began to nibble it.

High in the old pine tree, a snowy owl looked out across the still, white meadow. He spread his great wings and sailed upward.

"Whooo—whoo—whoo—," he called softly.

The little mouse heard the hunting cry of the owl. She darted for the safety of the stone wall. She crouched, waiting. Her small body shook with fear and hunger.

A snowshoe rabbit huddled near. One of its long ears bent forward. Quickly, in zigzagging leaps, he bounded away.

For a while the mouse stayed close to the stone wall. But something began to trouble her. She had been away from her nest for too long. Even though she

87

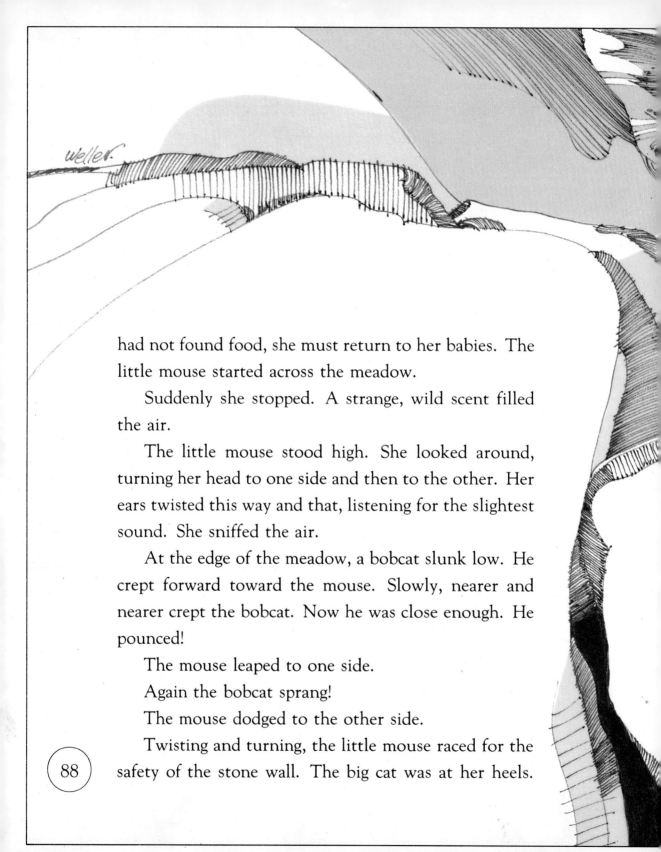

had not found food, she must return to her babies. The little mouse started across the meadow.

Suddenly she stopped. A strange, wild scent filled the air.

The little mouse stood high. She looked around, turning her head to one side and then to the other. Her ears twisted this way and that, listening for the slightest sound. She sniffed the air.

At the edge of the meadow, a bobcat slunk low. He crept forward toward the mouse. Slowly, nearer and nearer crept the bobcat. Now he was close enough. He pounced!

The mouse leaped to one side.

Again the bobcat sprang!

The mouse dodged to the other side.

Twisting and turning, the little mouse raced for the safety of the stone wall. The big cat was at her heels.

She was almost to the wall.

With a great bound, the bobcat leaped forward.

The mouse felt sharp claws rake her fur. End over end, she somersaulted across the snow.

In a last, desperate leap, the mouse sprang for the wall. She squeezed herself into a crack between the stones.

The cat pushed a paw inside. His sharp claws stretched toward the mouse, but he could not reach her. The little mouse was safe.

With an angry snarl the bobcat turned and trotted away.

Her narrow escape and her hunger had exhausted the mouse. Her strength was almost gone. She was too weak now to return to her nest and her young.

She lay huddled against a rock, her small sides heaving.

She rested.

She nibbled a dry tuft of grass wedged between the stones. It was not much but it helped to fill the hollow place in her empty stomach. With her forepaws she pulled at the grass.

Suddenly, out of the crack between the stones, spilled acorns and weed seeds. It was a squirrel's forgotten storehouse of food.

Today the little mouse was lucky.

She ate and ate until her small stomach could not hold one single seed more. Then she stuffed her cheeks full. Away she raced. Back to her tunnel in the snow she went—back to her nest and her family.

With tiny squeaks of delight, the mouse-babies welcomed their mother. She pulled them close.

When their stomachs were stretched tight with the warm milk, the mouse-babies snuggled into their mother's shaggy fur. Safe and warm in their cozy nest, the mouse-babies went to sleep.

Focus

1. The bear mouse set out to get food. What happened to her on the way?
2. How did the mouse's size help her escape from the bobcat?
3. What had the squirrel forgotten that helped the mouse?
4. What senses did the mouse use?

91

The bear mouse lives in a home under the ground. You can discover where other animals spend their lives.

ANIMAL HOMES
SALLY CARTWRIGHT

A Home above the Ground

A gray squirrel makes a winter home in a hollow tree. She lines her hole with moss, grass, and leaves. In the spring, safe in her warm nest, the mother squirrel gives birth to about five tiny babies. They have no fur and their eyes are closed. They are helpless. In four weeks their eyes open. Their fur has grown, and they will have bushy tails.

When they are too big for their snug little hole, they move to a summer home. It looks like a large ball

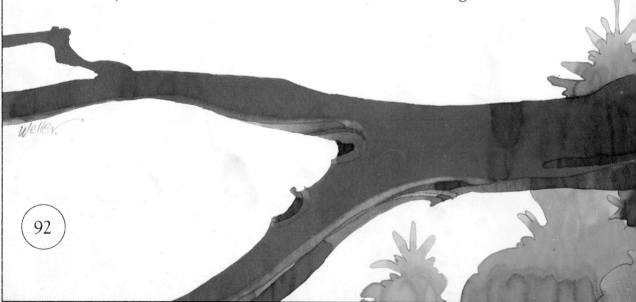

of dead leaves high in the tree. A squirrel builds this hollow ball of sticks and leaves. Inside there is a soft floor of moss. This summer home is safe for the squirrel family.

When fall comes, a gray squirrel makes its winter home in a hollow tree again. It is safe and warm through the snow and winds of winter.

A squirrel gathers seeds and nuts. It hides them under roots and leaves and stones. It may sleep on the coldest days of winter. On sunny days it climbs down to dig out some of its food. It is watchful and nimble and quick. It is always ready to dash up to its home for safety.

A Home on the Ground

A baby porcupine is born in late spring. The baby is big and strong when it is born. It looks like its mother. Its eyes are open. It is covered with black hair and has sharp quills, like knitting needles, hiding in its hair.

When the porcupine is only two days old, it can climb a tree. It is born when the weather is warm, so it does not need a cozy home. The little porcupine is protected by its quills. It waddles along slowly, and it does not need to run and hide. It turns its tail toward a dog or other animal . . . and just waits.

The quills stand up, bristling and dangerous. The porcupine can lash its tail and strike a dog or person, but it cannot shoot its quills. When touched, the quills

can come loose. Their barbed points stick into the other animal.

By the end of summer the young porcupine has grown almost as large as its mother. It leaves her and lives by itself. In winter the porcupine spends much of its time in the top of an evergreen tree. It eats the inner bark and twigs. Sometimes it hurts the tree by taking too much bark with its strong front teeth.

Sometimes it sleeps in the tree. It looks like a furry black lump high in the branches. On the ground it may find a rocky niche for a den. It is not very friendly, but it may sleep with other porcupines for warmth during winter. A porcupine home is not easy to find because it is so simple. If you do find a mother porcupine at home, stay clear of those quills!

A Home under the Ground

The woodchuck builds its home underground. Its large front feet and strong claws are thick and powerful for digging. Its legs are short for going down tunnels. Often the woodchuck digs its home in an open field. It may be near a berry patch or vegetable garden where the woodchuck eats its meals. Its home is easy to find. It is marked by a pile of dirt, which the woodchuck has pushed from its hole.

The woodchuck digs a tunnel until it gets about four feet below the ground. There the woodchuck makes a room for its nest. Then the animal digs more tunnels. These tunnels end in rooms for storing winter food.

The woodchuck makes a secret back door. If you could measure the tunnels of one woodchuck home, they would add up to anywhere from twenty to forty feet.

The woodchuck brings leaves and grass in its teeth. It lines its nesting room to make it soft and warm and dry. The woodchuck will sleep through the winter there. The woodchuck sleeps very soundly. Even if you shook it with your hands, you could hardly wake it. Its home is far underground, where no harm can come while it sleeps.

This long winter sleep is called *hibernation*. In late summer the woodchuck eats a lot and gets fat. Around October, when the weather turns cold, it waddles into its den, curls up snugly, and falls into deep sleep. The woodchuck's heartbeat slows down. Its breathing slows down. Its body cools down.

In February the coldest part of winter is over. The woodchuck wakes up.

In the spring, the mother woodchuck has from two to eight tiny woodchucks. Like squirrels, they are unseeing and helpless. Their mother keeps them warm and safe underground. She brings them clean, soft grass and feeds them her milk.

Baby woodchucks open their eyes about one month after they are born. By now they are furry and active. They wiggle up the tunnel and see daylight. They eat tender grass and leaves. They learn to sit up and watch for danger.

They stay with their mother a few more weeks. By the end of the summer they are big and fat. Their front paws have grown strong and powerful. They dig their own homes, where they will hibernate for the winter.

Animal Homes

Each home is right for the animal that uses it. Each home is built where the animal finds safety, food, and shelter for its babies.

Porcupine homes are right on the ground. Woodchuck homes are under the ground. The squirrel, who is fast, safe, and sure in the trees, makes its home above the ground.

Most animal homes are made for many reasons. They make a safe place for the babies. Many of the homes also keep the grown animals warm and dry. Animals have learned to hide their homes well.

Focus

1. Gray squirrels make a winter home and a summer home. How are they different?

2. Porcupines do not build a nest. Where do they live? What defenses do they have?

3. Where does the woodchuck make its home? Describe the woodchuck's home.

4. How are the different homes suited to the different animals?

STUDY SKILL: Alphabetical Order

Suppose you want to make up a list of the animals you have studied. The list might look like this:

mouse
porcupine
squirrel
woodchuck

How are the words in the list arranged? They are in alphabetical order. The first letter of each word follows the order of the alphabet. Where would the word *owl* fit in this list?

Why would you alphabetize your list? Let's say the class has studied many animals. It has a long list. You want to know if anyone has read about giraffes. If the list is in alphabetical order, it will be easy to find the word you want.

Knowing your ABCs can help you in other ways. It can help you to find a name in the phone book or a word in the dictionary. Both these books are alphabetized.

You may have to look past the first letter to alphabetize words. Two words may have the same first letter. They may have the same first and second letters. To put them in order, you have to look at the third letter in each word.

Look at these words:

baboon
bald eagle
bantam rooster
bat

What letters are the same in all these words? Where would you add *bass* to this list? Where would you add *badger?*

Use what you have learned to answer these questions. Write your answers on a sheet of paper.

1. Tell when you might alphabetize words.
2. How is the phone book arranged?
3. Suppose you want to alphabetize the words *like* and *list.* Which word would come first?
4. Alphabetize these words:
   moose   monkey   mole   mouse   mockingbird

Animals use their senses to find food and make homes. People do something more. They often make friends of the other people who live near them.

Gifts
of Laughter
BEVERLY V. HURLBUT

My father and I walk to Old-Man-Appa's house. It is getting dark outside, and the road through the desert is dusty. There is only enough sunlight to see the brown dust puff around our feet. Each step makes another brown puff. I wish it would rain so the land would not be so dry. The small stalks of corn look thirsty.

Every day I hurry home after school so I can go with my father. Sometimes we walk through the village roads. Sometimes we drive. Some days we drive out to see if the grass and corn are growing. My father wants to see if there will be winter feed for the animals.

He stops to talk to the Zuñi people. I like to watch my father talk, and I listen to what he says. He talks to them in the Zuñi language. The Zuñi men and women

talk quietly to my father. Sometimes I can hardly hear what they say, but my father always hears them. There is a lot of laughter and I laugh, too. I listen to the laughter, and I think that's what I will do when I grow up.

While my father talks to the men and women, I talk to the other children. Sometimes they just peek around their mothers at me. But when I smile at them, they always smile back. My father makes more jokes. We all laugh again.

As we walk to Old-Man-Appa's house, I think of people laughing. It is good to make people happy, I think. The sound of laughter is a good sound. We are going to Old-Man-Appa's house to see if he is well. He has been sick and my father has not seen him for a few days.

My father knocks on Old-Man-Appa's door. The old man opens the door. My father says "Hello!" to him in Zuñi. Old-Man-Appa shakes my father's hand.

"*Emu*," he says. In the Zuñi language, this means "Sit down."

My father and I sit beside the table where Old-Man-Appa works. He has been making jewelry. There are strips of silver on the worktable. There are pieces of sky-blue turquoise. The Zuñi people think that the turquoise stones are the most beautiful things in the world. I think so, too.

On the work table are lots of rings. One of them is shaped like a butterfly. It is beautiful! In my mind, I can see it fly up . . . up . . . up. Old-Man-Appa sees me looking at the ring. Quietly he picks it up and puts it on my finger.

"It fits. It fits!" I say to myself.

My father smiles at me. "How much?" he asks Old-Man-Appa.

When Old-Man-Appa shakes his head, I feel great sadness. He does not want to sell this ring.

"No," says Old-Man-Appa. "I will not sell this ring. In town, I sell my cows and sheep. In town, I sell my other silver jewelry. This ring I will not sell."

Old-Man-Appa looks at my father, then he looks at me. He smiles. "But I will give it to you, because you are my friend."

Everyone laughs. The laughter shows that we are friends.

Focus
1. Name two things that tell what the desert is like.
2. Why did the Zuñi like the father in this story?
3. What was the reason for the visit to Old-Man-Appa?
4. There are two gifts in this story. What are they?

To capture the flight of a butterfly in silver—what a lovely thing to do! What is it like to work in silver?

Zuñi Silversmith

HELEN M. JONES

The jeweler sits at her worktable, checking each new stone in turn. She has a design in mind. Now she needs an unusual stone to carry it out.

That morning, while walking, she had seen the design. The sharp rays of the sun had cast a hard-edged shadow. The shadow curved from the edge of a rock, away across the sand.

As soon as she got back from her walk she drew the design. It was the curve she liked, the graceful curve of sand that bent the straight edge of the rock. She made eight drawings. Each said something different about the meeting of sun and rock and sand. She might use them all some day, but for this piece she had picked the one she wanted.

Three stones get chosen from the lot. They are checked for weight and feel. When they are shaped and polished, will the highlights of color fall in the right place? Is there a flaw to work around? One is right; the rest are put aside.

The jeweler goes back to the drawing. The design needs to be rounder in one spot to fit the shape of the stone. She draws again. This time she likes what she sees.

She moves to her workbench. There, waiting for her, are her tools and the supply of silver. She opens the locked chest. There is the fine wire that will become the chains for necklaces. There is the heavier wire that will be turned into rings or bracelets. There are the sheets of silver, ready to be cut. And there are the scraps from other work she has done.

The jeweler calls these scraps her friends. They all will be used in some way. Sometimes, like a good friend, the scraps surprise her. They may help her discover a new way to work the gleaming metal.

Her tools wait for her, too. She can reach each one without looking. She knows what each will do to the silver. A flat area of silver, with no design in it, will

gleam like the huge blue desert sky with no clouds. A piece of silver with designs hammered in it will sparkle like a star-filled sky at night.

The jeweler starts to work. There, in the scrap-pile, lies a sheet of silver large enough to take the design. She is going to make a pendant for a necklace. It's going to be quite large, and this piece of silver has the weight she wants. She smiles. Her friend, this scrap, has changed her plan a bit. The pendant starts to take on its own life, as she works.

The jeweler heats the metal, then starts to shape and bend it. The straight edge starts to take the curve she wants. She shapes, and heats, and shapes again.

The day goes on. Step by step she works the silver, then the stone. Then she works the silver again. This pendant will soon be done. It will join the other works of art that earned her the title Zuñi Master Jeweler.

Focus

1. Where did the silversmith get the idea for the pendant?
2. Once she had the idea, what did she do next?
3. What did the silversmith check for in the stones?
4. What did she do after she had picked the stone?
5. List the other steps she used to make the pendant.
6. What other craftspeople might work like this?

Before You Came This Way

You walk
down this canyon,
this place of
high red cliffs
and turning winds
and hawks that float
in a far white sky
and
you wonder:
"Am I the first one
ever
to come this way?"

And
you wonder:
"Is my footprint
the first one
ever
to touch this sand?"

But
then you see something
which tells you,
No,
you're not the first.
Your brothers
out of some
long ago lost age
passed this way too.

You see their marks
on canyon walls.
Even the print
of their hands
is left,
chipped deep
in stone.

These men
who came before you—
    cliff dwellers,
    hunters,
    wanderers—
    left messages
    on rocks,
    on cliff sides,
    on steep rough
    canyon walls.

They drew
the things
they did
and saw.
They even drew
their corn plants

and the birds
that flew above
their heads
and the paths
men cut
through nameless lands.

BYRD BAYLOR

111

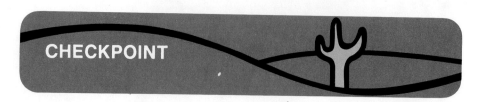

CHECKPOINT

Find the best word to fit the sentences. Write the sentences on your paper. Write new sentences for the extra words.

moss   desert   underground   forward

silver   exhausted   huddled   squirrel

1. Cactus plants grow best in the _____.
2. The baby birds _____ together in their nest.
3. My ring is made of _____.
4. Take two steps backward and one step _____.
5. Some _____ was growing on the side of the tree.
6. We watched a _____ gather nuts for the winter.

Read the paragraphs below. Then answer the questions that follow. Write the correct answers on your paper.

The bear mouse was hungry. Her food supply was gone. She left her nest because she had to find food.

At last she came upon some nuts hidden in a wall. She ate a few of them and filled her cheeks with the rest. She had to go back to her nest to feed her babies.

7. Why was the bear mouse hungry?
8. Why did the mouse leave the nest?
9. Why did the mouse fill her cheeks with nuts?

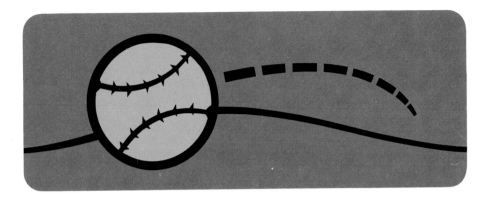

Choose the right word to complete each sentence. Write each sentence on your paper.

trust—distrust   like—dislike   appear—disappear

10. I _____ the weak legs on that old chair, so I won't sit in it.

11. I'm glad I made the team; I really_____playing softball.

12. The tree seemed to _____ in the fog.

Put these animal names in alphabetical order. Then answer the questions on your paper.

cormorant   aardvark   emu   alpaca
copperhead   adder   puffin

13. What is the first name on your list?

14. Which comes first, *cormorant* or *copperhead*?

15. After which word would you put *codfish*?

113

People often make friends with other people. Hubert
enjoys his pet goat.

The Goat That Went to School, Part 1

ELLIS CREDLE

The clouds hung heavy about the mountains.
Hubert could step outside the cabin and wash his face
in their damp, white mist. That was how high up he
lived. His little log house was built on the steep side of
old Thunderhead Mountain. The houses down in the
village seemed smaller than matchboxes. It was easy to
pick out the schoolhouse from the others. Its new tin
roof glittered in the sun and sent up shafts of light like
a diamond.

Hubert sat on a rock ledge in front of his home. He
stared down at the bright roof longingly. He was ten
years old and he had never been to school.

114

It took a whole day to get to school by the road. But Hubert knew a short cut. It was a steep path, zigzagging down the face of the mountain. Hubert could make it in an hour.

He pleaded with his mother to let him go to school. She always said, "I'm afraid for you to walk it alone in the wintertime. If the snow began to fly, pretty soon the trail would be covered. You'll not be able to decide which way to turn. You'd wander on the mountains until you were lost and frozen with the cold. No, you'll have to make do with what your dad and I can teach you."

"Can't I just start this year?" begged Hubert. "I could go until the days begin to get cold and it looks like snow."

"Well, I guess there would be no harm in that," said his mother. "You can go during the month of September. There's never any snow in September." Hubert was joyful. Even one month in school was something to look forward to.

Now Hubert began to worry about his clothes. All he had to wear was a pair of blue overalls and a homespun shirt. The other boys in the school would have on store-bought pants and nice striped shirts. Then there were books. Where would he get the money for books?

If there were only a way he could earn a little money! Hubert thought and thought. One day he said to his mother, "I think I'll go ask Mr. Honeycutt if he would like some help picking his apples. Maybe I could make a little money to buy some store clothes and some books."

"Go right ahead," his mother nodded. "Asking won't hurt."

Hubert set off around the mountain to his neighbor's farm.

"Why, yes, I can use a little help loading my apples," said Mr. Honeycutt.

Hubert set to work. He picked up the sound apples from the ground. He plucked the ripe ones from the tree. Then he helped Mr. Honeycutt to lift them into his wagon. When it was loaded high, Mr. Honeycutt hitched up his old brown mule. Then he climbed into the driver's seat.

"I'll not forget you when I sell my apples in the town," he promised. "I'll be back in two or three days.

I'll stop by your house with your pay."

On the third day Hubert heard Mr. Honeycutt's wagon coming.

"Whoa!" cried Mr. Honeycutt, with a smile. "Well, Hubert, I've got your pay!"

He must have got a good price! Maybe he's going to pay me a lot, thought Hubert. He ran out to the covered wagon.

Mr. Honeycutt leaned into the back of the wagon. He began to pull something forward. "Well, here's your pay. How do you like it?"

Out peeped a neat, fur-covered head with two dainty horns. It was a goat!

"Well, how do you like him?" he asked. "He cost more than I ought to pay for having my apples picked. But then I remembered how a boy loves a goat."

Though Hubert was surprised, it would not do to let Mr. Honeycutt see that he would rather have the money. Besides, it was a pretty, neat-looking little goat and he had always wanted one.

17

"Oh, Mr. Honeycutt, he sure is a fine goat. I thank you, I sure do!" Hubert took the goat's rope. The trim little animal bounded out of the wagon.

"Land sakes! What have you got there?" asked his mother.

"Well, I've got a goat, though it's not what I expected. It's my pay for picking Mr. Honeycutt's apples."

"But I thought you wanted some money to get yourself some clothes."

"It's what he brought me," said Hubert. "I'd as soon have him."

The goat made himself right at home. Hubert fixed him a nice bed of leaves in a corner of the wood shed. He fed him some corn or oats every day and let him crop the grass in front of the cabin.

The goat was never too busy eating to stop to play with Hubert. He was frisky and full of fun. He would rear up on his hind legs and butt at Hubert playfully. When Hubert bent over, the goat ran at him from behind and sent him tumbling.

One time he did it when Hubert was pouring a bucket full of buttermilk for the pigs. Over Hubert went, sprawling into the trough full of buttermilk. He

went squishing and squashing to the house. There were streams of buttermilk running from his clothes, from his hair, and even from his ears.

Hubert's mother saw what the goat had done. She said, "That goat's going to be a nuisance. You had as well take him down to town and sell him. Then you'd have the money to buy your things."

Hubert shook his head. Naughty as the goat was, Hubert had learned to love him. Hubert didn't like to think of selling him, even for some clothes and his books. There must be another way of making a little money.

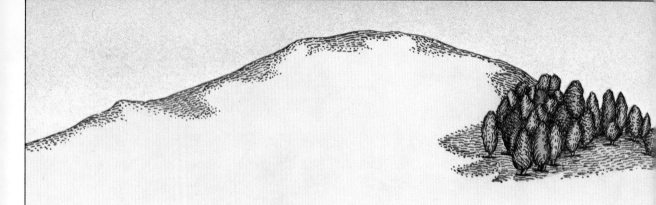

The next day he tried to think of another way to earn some money. "I think I'll go pick berries," he said to his mother. "Maybe I can pick enough to sell in the town. Then I could buy my things."

"It's worth trying," said Mother.

Before he left, Hubert took a stout piece of rope and tied the goat to a tree. "You'd best stay here where you'll be out of mischief," he said.

Off he started with a big basket over his arm. He was only halfway there when he heard a noise behind him. He turned and looked. There was the goat tripping up the steep stony trail. He was dragging his rope all frayed and chewed.

Focus

1. Hubert wanted to enroll in school, but he was not allowed to. Why not?
2. How did Hubert get the goat?
3. Why did Hubert decide to keep the goat?
4. How did the goat get loose?

The Goat That Went to School, Part 2

"How did you get loose?" cried Hubert. Just the same, he was half-glad to see his friend. All day long he picked berries. The goat was as good as could be. When his basket was full, Hubert set off for home.

"Come and see!" he cried when he got there. "Come and see how many berries I've got. And they're nice ones. I'll get a good price for them." He set his basket on the edge of the porch and ran to find Mother.

When he got back, he found the basket tipped over. His berries were spilled on the ground and all scuffed and crushed. The goat's mouth was stained with blackberry juice.

"I told you so," cried Mother, when she saw it. "That goat is nothing but a nuisance. Why don't you take him down to the town and sell him?"

Hubert looked at his naughty goat. Perhaps he should take Mother's advice. He'd likely get enough money for the goat to buy everything he needed. But he hated to part with his pet.

"I think I'll give him another chance," he said.

For a while the goat would go along as good as gold. But then Hubert would think up a way to make a little money. And the goat would defeat all Hubert's chances.

So, on the first day of September, Hubert set off sadly for the school. He was wearing the same old homespun shirt and his old blue overalls. He left the goat at home shut up tight in the wood shed. But not quite tight enough. When he was only halfway down the mountain he heard a quick trip-tripping behind him. He looked around and there was the goat prancing merrily after him.

Hubert frowned at him. "How did you get loose this time? If it hadn't been for you, I would have new pants and a nice, striped shirt," he said. "And I would have had some books to study from."

"Baa, baa, baa!" bleated the goat gaily. Down, down, down, they wound. At last they came to the school.

"Oh, look!" cried the children. "A new boy . . . and he has a goat!" They crowded around Hubert. No one noticed his faded shirt and his old blue overalls. They were much too busy asking about the goat.

When the school bell rang, the goat lay down on the porch. He waited while the children marched in for their lessons.

Hubert went uneasily. "What shall I do for books?" he thought. But as soon as he was seated, the teacher handed him a pile of them.

"They're yours for the year," she smiled at him. "The state gives us all our books. You're only supposed to keep them nice and clean. Next year another child can use them."

Every day for a month Hubert went down the trail to the schoolhouse. Every day the goat went merrily beside him. They did not mind the long hard trip. Hubert studied his lessons hard. He knew that cold weather was likely to come soon. He wanted to learn as much as he could.

If only he could keep on going to school. Perhaps
he could think up a way. But think as he would, not an
idea came.

Then came the end of September. It was his last day
in school. Hubert told his friends good-by and started
sadly for home.

Hubert climbed slowly up the mountain. He
noticed that the sky was dark and leaden. He was not
halfway home when soft flakes began to float down.
Snow in September! It couldn't be! The white flakes
flew thicker and thicker. Hubert hurried his footsteps.
He remembered what his mother had said about getting
lost.

Everything looked unfamiliar. He couldn't tell
which way to go. Any way he turned might start him
rambling. Then he would be lost in a snowstorm on
Thunderhead Mountain.

But the goat seemed not to have a worry in his
head. He frolicked ahead, bleating at Hubert, "Baa, baa,
baa!" Now and then, he returned to nip at Hubert's

pants. It was as though he were saying, "Come on, what are you waiting for?" It gave Hubert a glint of hope.

Perhaps he knows the way, Hubert thought. He put his hand on the goat's smooth back. They climbed and climbed. Hubert kept his eyes half-closed to keep the snow from blinding him. He did not know where he was going. But the goat was sure of the ground. At last Hubert felt himself on a level place.

Could they have reached the cabin? Hubert's heart gave a leap. He peered about. He could just make out a building. It was—yes, it was the cabin! He broke into a run.

When he pushed open the door, his mother looked up. She cried, "Hubert!" She hugged him tight. "Your dad was just setting off to look for you! I was afraid you were lost in the snow!"

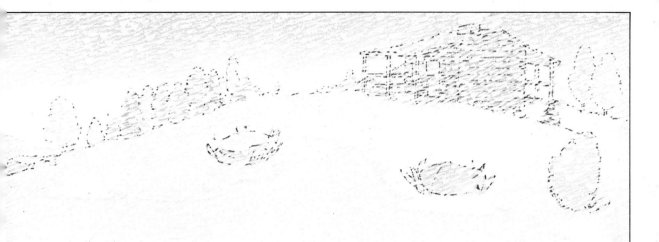

"Not with a goat like this!" cried Hubert. He opened the door wide so that his pet could come in. "I couldn't tell where to turn. But he stepped right out and led me straight along home!"

"That goat could lead you through anything," his father said. "You never need fear getting lost between here and the schoolhouse."

"I reckon you're right," agreed Mother.

After that there was nothing to keep Hubert from going to school during the rest of the year.

Focus

1. How did the goat defeat Hubert's chances to make some money?

2. How did the children at school feel about the goat?

3. Hubert was loyal to his pet goat. How did the goat help Hubert?

Hubert's goat could do something Hubert couldn't do. Bats use their senses in a way that people can't, too.

BATS IN THE DARK

JOHN KAUFMANN

Bats are different from birds. Bats have fur on their bodies instead of feathers. Their wings and tails are made of leathery skin stretched across thin bones.

Bats do not lay eggs, as birds do. Bat babies are born alive, the same way kittens are. Mother bats nurse their young with their own milk. That is why bats— like mice, cats, cows, and people—are called mammals. Of all the mammals, bats are the only ones that can truly fly.

Most bats are awake at night and asleep during the day. Near sundown they wake up and flutter around in their roosting places in old houses and caves. At nightfall they fly out to hunt for food. At daybreak they return.

One kind of bat is the little brown bat. Little brown bats and most other small bats are insect eaters. They catch flies, beetles, and moths in the air.

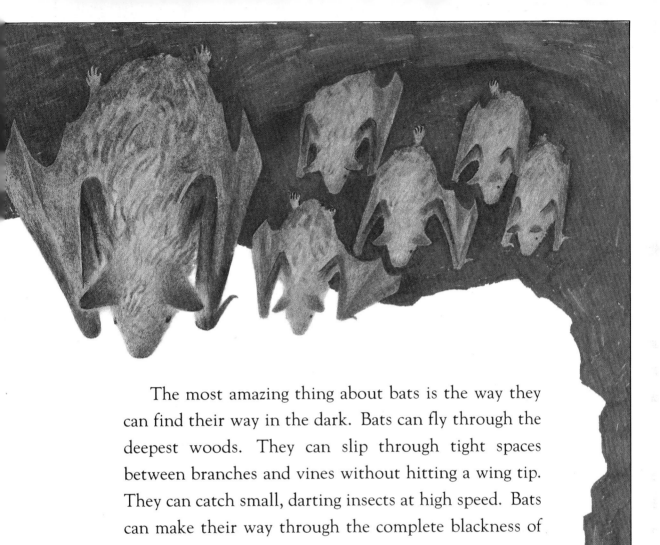

The most amazing thing about bats is the way they can find their way in the dark. Bats can fly through the deepest woods. They can slip through tight spaces between branches and vines without hitting a wing tip. They can catch small, darting insects at high speed. Bats can make their way through the complete blackness of deep caves.

Most bats do not use their eyes when they fly and hunt. To test this, scientists put blindfolds on bats. The bats could still find their way around. Then the scientists took the blindfolds off and covered the bats' ears. The bats bumped into things and could not catch insects. This showed that hearing is more important to bats than seeing. The bats were finding their way by listening to sounds!

A bat sends out sounds from its mouth. The sounds spread out through the air in waves. The sound waves keep going until they hit something, like an insect or a tree. Then the sounds bounce back to the bat as echoes. Different things make different echoes. By decoding these echoes, a bat can tell where it is flying. It can tell where the insects are.

When a bat hunts for food, it first sends out slow, putt-putt signals. When insect echoes bounce back, the bat speeds up the signals.

As they fly, bats seem to flip-flop in the air. This is because they turn quickly and spin around while chasing insects. Bats are so quick, they can catch two flies in one second. With the flick of a wing tip they can toss flies toward their tails. Their tails scoop the insects into their mouths. Bats are really expert acrobatic fliers.

There are many different kinds of bats. Some are very small. The largest ones have a wingspread of five feet.

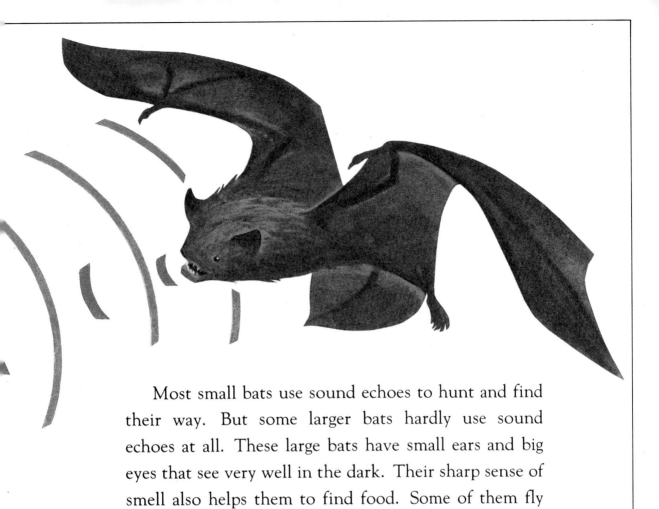

Most small bats use sound echoes to hunt and find their way. But some larger bats hardly use sound echoes at all. These large bats have small ears and big eyes that see very well in the dark. Their sharp sense of smell also helps them to find food. Some of them fly during the daytime.

People have trouble moving around in the dark. Bats' ears enable them to get along very well. A bat almost never bumps into anything in the dark.

Focus

1. Name three ways bats are different from birds.
2. Most bats use their ears as they fly. How did scientists discover this?
3. Tell how a bat uses its sense of hearing when it flies.

131

SCIENCE READING: What's It All About?

Echoes help bats to find their way. You can learn more about echoes from science books.

TAKE A FIRST LOOK

Part of a science book is printed on the next page. What is the page about? How many headings are there?

The side of the page is called the *margin.* Notes in the margin are called *marginal notes.*

FIND THE KEY IDEAS

What can you learn from the headings? Which headings go with the pictures on the page?

Find the words in **dark letters.** These words may be new to you, so their meanings are given in marginal notes.

READ CAREFULLY

You can get the meaning of new words from the way they are used. Also, use the pictures to help explain new words. You may need to read the page twice. Write the new words in a sentence.

ECHOES

How Echoes Start

Place your fingers against your throat while you talk. You will feel your throat moving back and forth. This movement is called **vibration.** Vibrations make the air move. This kind of air vibration is called a **sound wave.** Sound waves travel through water, too.

Suppose you shout across a valley. The sound wave hits the far side of the valley and bounces back. The returning sound wave is called an *echo.*

How Echoes Are Used

People use echoes. An echo system called **sonar** tells sailors when the water is deep enough for a boat. Sonar locates things under water, too.

Bats and dolphins use an echo system. It helps bats when they fly in the dark. Dolphins use it when swimming through dark water.

These animals make sounds. Then they listen for the echoes when the sounds bounce off objects. In this way the animals can locate the objects.

vibration
(vī brā′shən)
rapid back and forth movement

sound wave
vibration of air or liquid that is heard as noise

sonar (sō′när)
system that uses echoes to find objects in air or water

133

Most bats cannot see very well. However, the guards in this story think they can see very well.

Gillespie and the Guards

BENJAMIN ELKIN

In a country far away from here, there were three brothers. They could see better and farther than anyone else in the world.

The youngest brother had very powerful eyes. From a block away, he could read the date on a penny that was inside your pocket.

The middle brother had extra-powerful eyes. From two blocks away, with his eyes closed, he could see a tiny speck in the eye of a baby butterfly.

The oldest brother had super-extra-powerful eyes. In the darkest part of the night he could cover his face with a heavy bandage. He could still read every page of a closed book that was in a locked room three blocks away.

When the king heard about these wonderful brothers, he invited them to join the Royal Guards. The king was so proud of them that he announced a contest.

"My new guards have the brightest eyes in the world," said he.

"Anyone who can fool all three of them will win a gleaming golden medal set with shimmering, shining diamonds."

What a wonderful prize! From all over the world, people began flocking to the palace. A boy disguised himself as a dog. He ran all around the palace grounds, yelping, "Bow-wow!" and "Arf-arf!"

A man disguised himself as a giant clock. He stood in the corner of the palace all day, saying "Tick-tock, tock-tock."

None of these people could fool the new guards. With one glance, the guards could see through any disguise. Hundreds and hundreds of people tried and failed. The three brothers began to grow more and more famous.

But now the brothers didn't know how to behave. "How are we supposed to act?" asked the youngest brother. "Are we supposed to smile and laugh, or look serious and proud?"

"I think we should be serious," replied the middle brother. "After all, we're important people now."

"You're right," agreed the oldest. "From now on, let's be serious and proud."

To everyone's surprise, the new guards began to point their noses higher and higher in the air. They began to smile less and less. This bothered many people. Most of all, it bothered a little boy named Gillespie. Gillespie came to the palace every day to play. Until now he had thought that the Royal Guards were his friends.

"I'll enter that contest and make those guards smile again," he thought to himself. Besides, it would be nice to win a gleaming golden medal set with shimmering, shining diamonds.

Later that afternoon it was time for Gillespie to go home. He came up to the gate, pulling a little red wagon. The wagon was piled high with leaves.

Gillespie had to hold the leaves with one hand while he pulled the wagon with the other.

The youngest brother was on guard at the gate. He tried to look serious, but he couldn't help smiling a little.

"Just a minute, Gillespie," he said. "What are you hiding under those leaves?" With his powerful eyes he looked through and through the leaves. To his surprise, he could see nothing that was worth anything.

"All right," said the guard at last. "You're foolish to pull a pile of leaves all the way home. You can find all you want right on your own block. Just to prove you're not fooling me, I'll write it down."

In the Royal Guard Book he wrote: "Gillespie took a load of leaves."

137

The next day Gillespie again came to the gate, pulling a little red wagon. Behind him was a trail of sand. The wagon was piled so high with sand that he could hardly move it.

The middle brother was on guard at the gate. He, too, could not keep from smiling.

"Just a minute, Gillespie," he said. "Isn't it silly to try to hide things under that sand?" With his extra-powerful eyes he looked through and through the sand. To his surprise, he could see nothing that was worth anything.

"All right," said the guard at last. "You're foolish to pull a pile of sand all the way home. You can find all you want right on your own block. Just to prove you're not fooling me, I'll write it down."

In the Royal Guard Book he wrote: "Gillespie took a load of sand."

The third day, on his way home, Gillespie was really working hard. He was tugging and pulling at a little red wagon that was packed with stones. The pile was almost as high as Gillespie's head. The stones jiggled and bumped in the wagon.

This time the oldest brother was on guard at the gate, and he actually laughed out loud.

"Just a minute, Gillespie," he said. "What are you hiding under those stones?" With his super-extra-powerful eyes he looked at the very insides of those stones and right through them. He could see nothing that was unusual.

"All right," said the guard at last. "You're foolish to pull a pile of stones all the way home. You can find all you want right on your own block. We have to enforce the rules. Just to prove you're not fooling me, I'll write it down."

In the Royal Guard Book he wrote: "Gillespie took a load of stones."

This sort of thing went on day after day after day.

The guards laughed at him more and more. But every day they would just write it down in the Royal Guard Book. Then they would let him go on home.

At last there came a day when Gillespie asked to see the king. "Please, Your Majesty," he said, "I have succeeded in fooling all three of your new Royal Guards. I should like to have my medal, if you don't mind."

"Oh, no!" the king laughed. "You haven't fooled anybody. I have checked the Royal Guard Book myself.

I know that everything you took has been written down. Look, I'll show you."

And the king showed Gillespie pages and pages of the book. "Gillespie took a load of leaves . . . a load of sand . . . a load of stones. . . ."

"But, Your Majesty," said Gillespie, "that's how I fooled the guards. I kept them busy checking on the worthless things. They didn't even notice the important things I borrowed. Will you come to my home? I shall be glad to show you."

The king ordered the royal coach to drive him to Gillespie's home. A whole parade marched right down Gillespie's street. Gillespie rode beside the king in the royal coach. The three guards proudly rode ahead. The band made beautiful noises. The children all cheered.

When they came to Gillespie's house, he took them all to his garage. "Your Majesty," he said proudly, "you remember that palace storeroom for all the toys? Well, I borrowed all these things from that storeroom. I took them right past the Royal Guards!"

The king and the guards and all the people stared through the open door.

The garage was filled with dozens and dozens and dozens of LITTLE RED WAGONS!

So the king himself presented Gillespie with the gleaming golden medal set with shimmering, shining diamonds.

The three brothers are still famous, but they don't worry any more about acting so serious and proud. They know that no one is so great that he can't be fooled once in a while.

Gillespie is pretty famous, too.

After all, it's not every boy who can walk around town wearing a gleaming golden medal set with shimmering, shining diamonds.

Focus

1. Why were the three brothers chosen to be guards?
2. What prize did the king offer to anyone who could outsmart the guards?
3. Once the guards became famous, they behaved differently. How did Gillespie feel about this?
4. Tell how Gillespie succeeded in outsmarting the guards.
5. What did the guards learn from Gillespie?

Once Upon a Tree

. . . Once upon a tree
I came across a time,
It wasn't even as
A ghoulie in a dream.

There was a mooly man
Who had a rubber hat
And funnier than that—
He kept it in a can. . . .

THEODORE ROETHKE

145

CHECKPOINT

Use the words below to fill in the blanks. On your paper write each sentence with the word that fits in it.

behave   succeeded   flakes   scientists   decide

Hubert   September   bleated   mammals   echoes

1. To make up your mind is to _____.

2. Little bits of snow are called _____.

3. The ninth month of the year is _____.

4. If you have done what you set out to do, you have _____.

5. Dogs, cats, and bats are three kinds of _____.

6. To act a certain way is to _____.

7. When a goat makes a sound, it is said to have _____.

8. _____ is a boy's name.

Across your paper write the headings "Animal Homes," "Animal Food," and "Animal Coats." List each of the words below under the correct heading.

insects   fur   tunnel   hair

nest   seeds   feathers   berries

quills   den   nuts   burrow

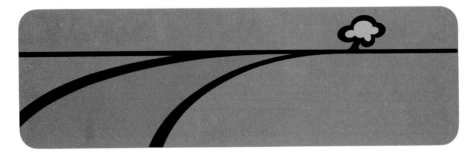

Read each sentence below. Decide what the cause is for each event. Write the whole sentences on your paper.

Comprehension:
Cause and Effect

9. The king gave Gillespie the medal because
   a. Gillespie was famous.
   b. Gillespie fooled the guards.
   c. Gillespie liked wagons.

10. Hubert got lost on his way home from school because
   a. the goat lost his way.
   b. it was snowing.
   c. he took a new road.

Use the two sets of words that follow to fill in the blanks in the sentences. Write them on your paper. Write your own sentences for the other words.

Decoding:
Prefixes
de-, en-

   code—decode   close—enclose

11. They wanted to _____ the yard by putting a fence around it.

12. He had to _____ the secret message to read it.

Dreamers and Do

The next group of stories is about different kinds of people. Some dream and find they can make their dreams come true. Others start out doing and keep doing more. Some of the characters, like Ben Franklin, really lived. Others, like Mateo and Caroline, are made up. But their discoveries are just as real as Ben's. As you read, you will make that discovery yourself.

ers

Once there was a boy who used common things in uncommon ways. His name was Benjamin Franklin, and he lived more than 200 years ago. Ben's father was a candlemaker. He wanted Ben to be one, too.

TOOLS FOR SWIMMING

JOHN TOTTLE

"What's in the box?"

John Collins and Ben Franklin were on their way to the Mill Pond for an evening swim. Ben had a wooden box under his arm. It was the kind he packed candles in.

"Oh, some things of mine," answered Ben. "And a big frog."

"You're funny, Ben. You catch frogs' eggs and carry them home. Then you carry the frogs back and turn them loose. Why not let the eggs alone and let the frogs grow up where they belong?"

Ben moved the box to his other side.

"I like to see them grow up. First you have a lot of

151

jelly with round eggs in it. After a while, every egg turns into a tadpole. Then you can watch the tadpoles for weeks as they change to frogs.

"When the frogs begin hopping around the house, my mother makes me let them go. I was going to save this one, but he's too big. He needs a real pond to swim in."

They had reached the path that led through the bushes to the water's edge. Pushing the branches to one side, Ben went down the path with his box. John followed.

They stopped at the shore of the pond. Ben set his box down in the tall grass. Raising the top of the box a crack, he reached inside.

Slowly he took out the frog.

"Watch," said Ben. He bent down and opened his fingers. The big frog hopped out over the water. There was a splash, and the frog swam out of sight.

"I wish people could swim as fast as that," said Ben. "They could, if they had what frogs have."

John saw a chance for an argument here. Both boys enjoyed debating, but John read grown-up books. He could always make his argument sound like things he had read.

"A frog doesn't have anything," he began. "Frogs swim well because that is their nature. Birds fly well;

frogs swim well."

Ben pulled off his shirt to get ready to swim. Suddenly he said, "I don't want to make candles when I grow up. I want to be a sailor." This sounded as though he were giving up the debate, but John knew better.

Ben said, "My father and I often take walks to see workmen. He hopes we may find a job I'll like more than sailing. Last week we watched bricklayers building a wall and people making furniture."

"What does all that have to do with frogs swimming?" asked John, getting ready to swim.

"I saw something," Ben went on. "When workers have a job to do, they decide what tool will do it best. Bricklayers could spread cement with almost anything. But they can spread it fastest with a tool made for the job."

"But we're talking about frogs!" said John. "They haven't any tools."

"Yes, they have. Didn't you notice my frog's big flat feet? They are just right for kicking against the water. If you had feet like his, you could swim as well as he does."

John laughed loudly. Holding his nose, he jumped into the water. When he came up, his long hair was straight and dripping. He shook it out of his eyes and

looked at Ben. Ben was putting flat pieces of wood on his bare feet.

Standing up in his new footwear, Ben went to the box. He took out two more boards. Each was about ten inches long and had a hole for the thumb. The boards looked like the kind that artists mix paints on.

"Now my feet and hands are almost as good as a frog's," Ben said.

"You won't be able to swim at all," laughed John, "but that wood should keep you floating. Come on in. I'll race you to the dam."

Ben waded into the water. He had tried his swimming tools in secret and liked them. The wooden feet gave him a strong kick. Holding the hand boards with his thumbs, he pushed them forward. They cut the water like knives. As he drew them back, he turned them so that their flat sides pulled against the water. He had never tested them for speed, but they might work.

"I'm ready, John," Ben said after a little practice. "I'll race you."

For half a minute, America's first frogman hoped to win. The extra pushing power helped, and Ben raced ahead. He tried to keep going. But the strain on his ankles and wrists was too much. After a while, he couldn't force himself to take another stroke.

John splashed ahead to the dam and got out of the water. Ben was splashing toward him.

"Tools don't help much after all," John shouted.

His friend let go of the hand paddles. He reached the dam and pulled himself up on it.

"The idea is right, but the tools aren't," he said. "A frog's feet are better made, and they are put on better."

Ben never forgot that swim. Neither did his friends. John told the other boys about Froggy Franklin's swim

157

across the mill pond. They kept the story going for days. Every evening someone would ask Ben how far he could hop, or how he was coming along with his croaking.

Ben took it good-naturedly. A joke was a joke, whether it was on him or someone else. He loved fun. But the idea behind his experiment was a serious one.

The idea could apply to anything. First you figured out how a thing worked. Then you tried to see how it could be done better.

Yes, it was a good idea. Too bad he had been defeated when he tried using it. Being the leader of his group meant a great deal to him. Now he saw that his standing had been hurt by failure with the swimming gear. Oh, well. Things would go better next time.

The next time came very soon. Ben and John Collins were spending a holiday in the woods. Their clothes lay in a heap on the bank of a pond. Before jumping in, Ben had tied the string of a large paper kite to a stick at the water's edge.

The wind was strong and a little cold when it touched his wet skin. But the water was warm.

Ben floated on his back and looked into the sky. He watched the kite. It looked very small, now, above the tree tops.

John stood up in the water, hugging his dripping

shoulders. "Ben," he called, "I'm going to dress."

Ben moved his arms and legs slowly, his eyes still on the kite. "Do me a great favor, will you, John?"

"What do you want? Hurry! I'm goose-pimples all over."

"Get my clothes, and carry them around to the big rock."

"I don't know about that. What are you going to do? Swim? It's at least a mile across the pond."

"Yes, I'm going to swim."

John's teeth had stopped chattering by the time he had dried off and slipped into his clothes. He was loosening the kite string when Ben ran up behind him.

"I'll take care of the kite," said Ben. He handed John the clothes. "Go on, John, please!"

John was not sure he wanted to take the clothes. There were times when you couldn't tell what Ben was up to.

Ben waited until John was out of sight. Then he untied the kite's string from the stick. The wind pulled hard at the kite. Ben was careful not to let the kite slip from his fingers.

Wading out to deep water and holding the stick at the end of the string, Ben lay back in the water. As soon as his feet were off the bottom, he began to move. He laughed out loud for joy. As he had hoped, the wind was taking him across the pond. It was taking him straight toward the big rock.

Now and again the string let up, and the kite started to drop. Ben found that he must hold back somewhat to keep the kite firmly against the wind. On he went like a sailboat!

At last the trip was over. Ben pulled in the kite and climbed up the rock. He sat there happily, kite in hand, and waited until John arrived.

The story of the ride filled John with wonder. "You're a clever fellow, and no mistake," he said.

Ben grinned. John Collins was clever himself. His praise meant a great deal. And Ben knew that word of his trip with the kite would spread. There would be no more laughing at Froggy Franklin.

Best of all, Ben proved to himself that his experiments could work. In the years to come they would take him a long way—much farther than across a pond.

Focus

1. Why did Ben and John go to the pond?
2. What did Ben discover from studying the frog?
3. Ben tried two experiments. Which one did not work? Why not?
4. Which experiment worked? Why did it work?

SOCIAL STUDIES READING: What's It All About?

When Ben Franklin grew up, he became famous. You may read about him in your social studies book. Here are some hints to help you read social studies books.

TAKE A FIRST LOOK

Look at the title on the next page. Look for headings and for words under the pictures. These words, called *captions,* will help you to understand the pictures.

FIND THE KEY IDEAS

Now read the headings and captions. You will find key words to help you understand the rest of the page.

READ CAREFULLY

There are many new ideas. Read the first paragraph and look for the main idea. Then read the first heading. What is the next part of the page about?

When you come to a new heading, stop reading. Think about the part you just read before you go on. You may need to read a part more than once. Study the pictures. Reread the captions. Doing these things will help you to understand your social studies book.

BENJAMIN FRANKLIN

Benjamin Franklin studied the way the world works. He tried out new ideas.

A Life-long Learner

Franklin proved that dark clothes feel warmer than light-colored clothes. He studied lightning. He found out that storms follow a pattern as they cross the land.

Franklin Finds Seashell Rocks on a Mountain

Once Franklin was on a mountain. He saw rocks made of seashells. But the sea was far away and much lower than the mountain. Franklin wondered how the shells got that high above the sea. He decided that many years ago the sea had covered the mountains.

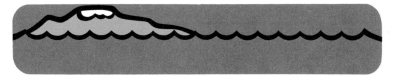

Franklin found seashell rocks high on a mountain.

We now know that Franklin's idea is one way to explain seashell rocks on a mountain. His ideas have helped us to learn about our world.

This is the kind of rock Franklin found. There are shells and parts of shells in it.

The rocks that Benjamin Franklin found are called fossils. One kind of fossil has seashells in it. Other kinds have plants or the bones of fish or animals in them.

Fossils Tell of Long Ago ALIKI

A huge fish was swimming around when along came a smaller fish. The big fish was so hungry it swallowed the little fish whole. The big fish died and sank to the bottom of the lake.

This happened ages ago. How do we know?

We know because the fish turned to stone. The fish became a fossil. A plant or an animal that has turned to stone is called a fossil.

Scientists can tell how old stones are. They could tell how old that fish fossil was. So we know that the fish lived ages ago.

How did plants and animals become fossils? Most plants and animals do not become fossils when they die. They rot, or they crumble, dry up, and blow away. No trace of them is left.

This could have happened to the big fish. We would never know it had lived. Instead, the fish became a fossil. This is how it happened.

When the big fish died, it sank into the mud at the bottom of the lake. Slowly the big fish rotted. Only its bones were left. The bones of the little fish it ate were left, too. The skeletons of the fish lay buried and

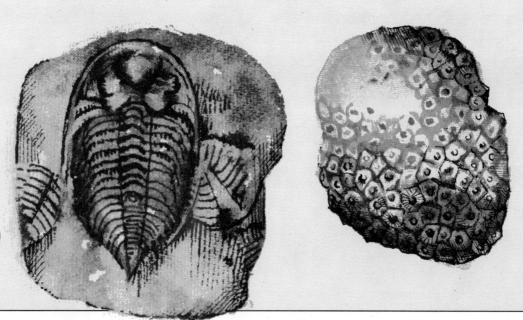

protected deep in the mud.

Years went by. More and more mud covered the fish. Tons and tons of mud piled up. After a long time, the surface of the earth changed. The lake in which the fish was buried dried out.

It rained on the drying mud. Water seeped through the mud. Minerals from stones were in the water. The water seeped into all the tiny holes in the fish bones. The minerals in the water were left behind in the fish bones.

After a very long time the minerals changed the bones to stone. The fish was a fossil. The mud around the bones became hard as rock, too.

Some fossils, like the fish, are bones or shells that have turned to stone. Sometimes a fossil is only an imprint of a plant or an animal.

Years and years ago a fern grew in a forest. It fell and was buried in muddy ground. The fern rotted away. But it left the mark of its shape in the mud. It left its imprint.

The mud got hard. The mud, with the imprint of the fern, became a fossil.

Fossils tell us there once were seas where now there are mountains. Fossils of sea plants and animals have been found on mountains.

How would you like to make a fossil? It won't be a years-and-years-old fossil, but a one-minute-old "fossil." Make a clay imprint of your hand, like this: Take some clay. Flatten it out. Press your hand in the clay. Lift your hand away.

Your hand is gone, but its shape is in the clay. You made an imprint. The imprint shows what your hand is like, the way the fern imprint shows us what the fern was like.

Suppose you buried your clay imprint when it dried. Suppose, a million years from now, someone found it. Your imprint would be as hard as stone. It would be a fossil of your hand. It would tell something about you. It would tell the person who finds it something about life on earth a million years earlier.

Focus

1. Name three things you learned about fossils.
2. Tell how the fish became a fossil.
3. What is the first thing you do when you make your own "fossil"? What is the last thing you do?
4. Name three types of fossils you might find in a good fossil collection.

ROCKS

Big rocks into pebbles,
pebbles into sand.
I really hold a million million rocks here in my hand.

FLORENCE PARRY HEIDE

"Fossils Tell of Long Ago" is about some uncommon rocks. An old folktale tells how people once used common rocks in an uncommon way.

STONE SOUP

JAMES BUECHLER

Characters:

CHIEF FORESTER

PETYA, a forester

SASHA, a forester

OLGA, a seamstress

VERA, a baker

DMITRI, a carpenter

ANNA

MARYA

Other VILLAGERS

Reprinted by permission from *Dramatized Folk Tales of the World*, edited by Sylvia E. Kamerman, Boston: Plays, Inc., Publishers. Copyright © 1971 by Plays, Inc. For reading purposes only; for permission to produce this play, write Plays, Inc., 8 Arlington Street, Boston, MA 02116.

171

Time:	Two hundred years ago.
Setting:	A village street in old Russia. Three houses stand along the street. Through large windows we see inside each house. There is a carpenter's shop, a bakery, and a seamstress' shop. There is a stream with stones on the right.
At rise:	Dmitri is at work in the carpenter's shop. Vera works in the bakery kitchen. Olga sits sewing in the seamstress' shop. Three foresters enter and walk down the street. Chief Forester carries an ax. Petya has a knapsack. Sasha carries a large cooking pot.

CHIEF FORESTER: (*To Petya and Sasha*) Cheer up, you two! We've come through the forest safely. I'm sure the people of this village will share their dinner with us.

SASHA: I hope so. My stomach is empty. It feels like a cave! (*Chief Forester knocks at Olga's door.*)

OLGA: (*Calling out of her window*) Who is it?

CHIEF FORESTER: It is only three foresters, walking home across Russia. Can you share some food, good woman?

OLGA: Food! No, I have nothing. Our harvest was bad. You will find nothing here. (*Turns from window*)

PETYA: (*Knocking at Vera's door*) Hello in there!

VERA: (*At window*) What is it you want?

PETYA: Some supper, if you have any. We are three hungry foresters walking home across Russia.

VERA: I am sorry to see you so hungry, but you have come to the wrong shop. It is everyone for himself in these times! (*Turns away*)

SASHA: (*Getting mad*) Let's see if our luck is better here. (*Knocks at Dmitri's door*)

DMITRI: (*Angrily*) Who are you, anyway? Smart men are inside their houses, working.

SASHA: We are three foresters, sir. It would be kind of you to share your dinner with us.

DMITRI: I have just enough dinner for myself. If I share, I eat one quarter of a dinner, and you get a quarter (*Pointing*), and so do you, and you. We shall all be hungry later. What good will that be? No, I do not believe in sharing. It is a very bad idea. (*Turns away*)

PETYA: What selfish people these are!

SASHA: (*Loudly*) They do not know how to share!

CHIEF FORESTER: Let's teach this one a lesson!

PETYA: No, no! We won't rob anyone.

CHIEF FORESTER: Of course not, Petya. All I meant was to teach these people to make Stone Soup.

SASHA: (*Catching on*) Ah, Stone Soup!

PETYA: (*Laughing*) That's just the thing! (*The three put their heads together, whispering. Dmitri comes to window again.*)

DMITRI: Are you still here? If you have no food, it's your lookout. Why aren't you on your way?

173

CHIEF FORESTER: (*Pretending not to hear*) Get some wood, Sasha! Get the kettle ready, Petya. We will build our fire here, on this spot. (*Sasha goes off left. Petya finds two Y-shaped sticks on the ground.*)

PETYA: We can use these to hang the kettle on. (*Sets sticks in place*)

CHIEF FORESTER: Perfect, Petya. Now for the stones. We must see if they have tasty stones in this village. Go and find some in that stream over there. (*Petya takes kettle to right. He throws some stones loudly into it. Olga and Vera turn and watch him from their windows. Sasha enters with dead branch.*) Good! That will burn well and heat our soup quickly.

SASHA: (*Lays fire, pretends to light it*) What kind of stones will we use for our soup today?

CHIEF FORESTER: What kind do you want?

SASHA: Oh, something filling! Granite is a good stone, now. I always like a granite soup. It has body. It sticks to your ribs! (*Petya brings kettle to center, rattling stones. Dmitri, Vera, and Olga leave houses, come near fire. Anna and Marya enter, followed by other Villagers.*)

DMITRI: (*Tugging Chief Forester's coat*) Pardon me.

CHIEF FORESTER: Eh? Oh, it is you, my friend.

DMITRI: What did you say you are cooking here?

CHIEF FORESTER: (*In an offhand way*) Just a stone soup. (*In a friendly way*) Tell me, what kind of stone do you like yourself? You might help us choose.

DMITRI: I! Why, I never heard of making soup from stones!

SASHA: You never heard of Stone Soup?

PETYA: I don't believe it.

CHIEF FORESTER: (*To Dmitri*) Come, sir. If you are not joking, you must eat with us. (*Petya shakes kettle.*) Have you some good stones there, Petya? Let Sasha choose.

SASHA: (*Examining stones*) Hm-m! This chunky one—it will be good! Washed down from the mountains, it has a

flavor of snow on it. Ugh! Throw that one away. A flat stone has a flat taste.

PETYA: How about the red one?

CHIEF FORESTER: No, no, that is only an old fireplace brick. It will taste like smoke. Nothing but fresh stones. We shall have a guest.

SASHA: Fill the kettle, Petya. My fire is ready. (*Petya dips water from well into kettle and hangs kettle over fire.*)

CHIEF FORESTER: (*To Dmitri*) Have you a spoon? We foresters often make do with a stick. But for a guest, the soup will need proper stirring and tasting.

DMITRI: I have just the thing. It has a nice long handle. It is like new. I have not had guests in five years.

CHIEF FORESTER: (*Clapping him on back*) Good work, you generous man! (*Dmitri goes inside for spoon.*)

ANNA: (*To Marya*) What's this? The foresters are making a soup from stones?

MARYA: (*Nodding*) Yes, stones from our own brook. That forester put them in. I saw him myself.

SASHA: (*Smelling the air*) Oh, it makes me hungry!

DMITRI: (*Returning with spoon*) Here you are. Please be careful.

CHIEF FORESTER: Sir, you shall be served first. (*Stirs, tastes*)

MARYA: I am very hungry. It must be the smell of this soup they are cooking.

ANNA: I must have a cold, for I can smell nothing.

MARYA: (*Sniffing*) Yes, I am very hungry! I have worked in the fields since morning, with no lunch, either. What good soup! (*Chief Forester, Sasha, and Petya each taste by turns, and lick lips.*)

OLGA: Is it good?

PETYA: Good!

DMITRI: Good? (*Reaches for spoon*)

SASHA: (*Keeping spoon away from him*) Oh, so good!

CHIEF FORESTER: It might stand an onion, though. Onion is very good for pulling the flavor from a stone.

OLGA: You know, I might find an onion in my house.

FIRST VILLAGER:	Hurry then, Olga. Get some. (*Olga exits.*)
SASHA:	(*Tasting*) Does it need just a touch of carrot, Mr. Forester? (*Villagers look at each other.*)
VERA:	Perhaps I could bring some carrots for this soup.
CHIEF FORESTER:	That is kind of you. And will you bring a bowl for yourself, as well? You must eat with us. (*Vera goes inside as Olga returns with onions.*)
OLGA:	Use what you like. I should like to learn to make this soup. (*Chief Forester adds onions, tastes. Petya tastes also.*)
PETYA:	Should we add just a bit of potato, perhaps? I cannot say that Stone Soup is ever quite right without a potato or two.
OLGA:	That is true. A stone is nothing without a potato! (*Vera returns with carrots and bowl. Chief Forester adds carrots.*)
MARYA:	(*To Villagers*) Vera was invited, did you hear? How can we be invited as well? (*They whisper together. Anna goes off right. Marya calls out.*) If you need some potatoes for that soup of yours, I have a sack in my house! (*Anna appears with sack. Marya and Anna give the sack to Chief Forester.*)
CHIEF FORESTER:	Many thanks. Please stay for dinner. And now, Sasha, let's get to business! (*Tasting*) Add a potato . . . another . . . another. (*Sasha is already ahead of Chief Forester's count.*) No, stop, Sasha. Stop!

179

DMITRI: What is the matter?

CHIEF FORESTER: Too many potatoes! The potatoes have soaked up the flavor of the stones.

VILLAGERS: (*Ad lib*) Oh, too bad! What a shame!

MARYA: Is there nothing we can do?

PETYA: I have an idea. Meat and potatoes go well together. Let's add some meat.

DMITRI: I have a ham that will do the job. Wait here. (*Goes inside*)

CHIEF FORESTER: It might work, at that. (*Dmitri returns with ham.*)

SECOND VILLAGER: Good for you, Dmitri!

FIRST VILLAGER: Quick thinking!

ALL: (*Clapping*) Hurrah, hurrah! (*Chief Forester adds ham.*)

MARYA: Can anyone make this Stone Soup?

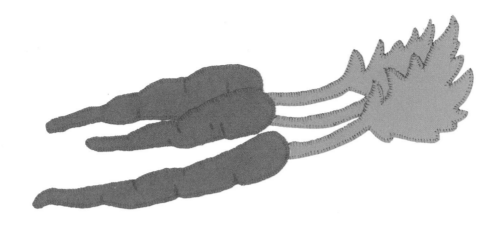

PETYA: Oh, yes. All you need are stones, fire, water—and hungry people.

ANNA: (*In a hurry*) Well, how is it now? It smells delicious.

CHIEF FORESTER: (*Tasting*) Hm. Some stones, as you may know, contain salt in them. These from your brook do not seem to be that kind. (*Olga goes inside.*)

OLGA: (*Returning*) Here is your salt. (*Chief Forester adds salt, with a big wave of his hand.*)

CHIEF FORESTER: Friends! Your attention, please! I know this will be a very good soup. You have fine stones in this village! Stay and eat with us, one and all. (*Villagers cheer and move about. First Villager goes offstage. She returns at once with bowls. Chief Forester fills them and all taste soup.*)

DMITRI: This is truly a delicious soup, folks!

ANNA: It has a good flavor!

MARYA: It fills you up!

DMITRI: And to think, neighbors, it's made only of stones! (*Foresters now move to stage front. They hold out their bowls of soup.*)

FORESTERS: (*To audience*) Yes, think of that! It's made only of stones!

(*Curtain*)

Focus

1. Why did the foresters decide to make Stone Soup?

2. Sasha said, "A flat stone has a flat taste." What does the second *flat* in that sentence mean?

3. What things were added to the stones to make the soup taste better? What would the soup taste like without them?

4. Do you think the villagers will try to make Stone Soup? Why or why not?

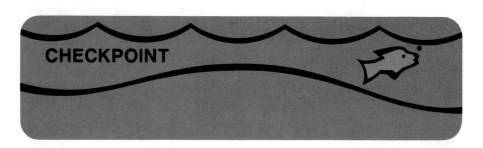

CHECKPOINT

Vocabulary: Word Identification

Below are five words. Each word is followed by three meanings. On your paper write the word and next to it the correct meaning.

1. kettle   (small cat; large pot; kind of tree)
2. wade   (walk quickly; walk backward; walk through water)
3. debating   (scolding; yelling; arguing)
4. seamstress   (one who sews; one who farms; one who fishes)
5. argument   (strange sight; disagreement; laughter)

Vocabulary: Vocabulary Development (connotations)

Read the sentences. Pick the words that make the most sense in the sentences. Write the sentences on your paper.

6. Ben was _____ when the kite pulled him across the pond. He knew he would be a hero to his friends.
   happy   thrilled   sad
7. The foresters had not eaten anything for three days. They were _____.
   full   hungry   starving

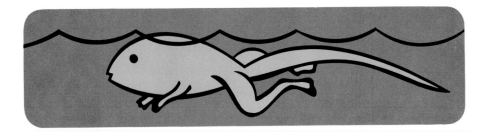

Some of the sentences that follow are facts. Others are opinions. Write the numbers on your paper. Next to each number write either the word *fact* or the word *opinion.*

Comprehension:
Fact and Opinion

8. Frog eggs turn into tadpoles.
9. Ben was foolish to try to swim like a frog.
10. Ben's kite pulled him through the water.
11. Scientists can tell how old some stones are.
12. It's fun to make an imprint.

Read the words below. On your paper, answer the questions that follow.

Decoding:
Suffix *-ion*

subtract   collect   correct
subtraction   collection   correction

13. Which word means "the act of taking one number away from another"?
14. Which word means "something that has been changed to make it right"?
15. Finish this sentence: My _____ of stones is not big enough; I am going to go _____ some more.

185

Both stones and clay come from the earth. "Stone Soup" was about people who used stones in an unusual way. In this story Mateo uses clay to make something beautiful.

THE CLAY HORSE

MARTHA GOLDBERG

One morning, just as the sun came up, Mateo brought the firewood down from the mountain.

The houses of Mateo's village were far below. Each family in the village made the black pottery that was famous over all of Mexico.

Mateo's mother was one of the finest potters in the village. Today she would fire the *ollas*—the large water jars. So Mateo hurried with the wood.

He also wanted to see Panchita, the beautiful brown horse. Panchita belonged to Big Pablo.

Mateo had often stopped to watch this beautiful horse. Then he had gone home and tried to make a horse from clay. His clay horses never looked like Panchita. Mateo wanted to see her again.

Mateo was sure that he could make a good clay horse. But that was a secret that no one knew, not even his sister, Concha.

When Mateo reached home his father called out, "Mama is waiting for the wood. Where have you been so long?"

"I stopped at Big Pablo's," Mateo answered.

"You stopped while we waited for you?" his father asked.

"Sí," Mateo said, all in a rush. "I stopped to see Panchita. Big Pablo told me he is selling her. Please, Papa, can we buy Panchita?"

"My son, don't be foolish! We are potters; we do not own horses. And today we have a lot of work to do. Let me hear no more about horses!"

Without a word Mateo put the wood in a neat pile. Then he went into the house for a lump of clay.

He began to work quickly with the clay. He rolled it into a ball. Then he wet his fingers and smoothed it. He made a head with tiny ears. Then he made the legs and tail of small rolls of clay.

He held up the little horse to look at it. It was not right. A horse was harder to make than a clay whistle or a bell. His mother had taught him to make those. But he knew he could make his horse now if there were time.

"Mateo! Mateo!" It was his mother calling him.

"I am here, Mama," he answered. Mateo held out the horse for her to see. "I was making this," he said. "I wanted to finish it."

Mama took the little horse in her hands. "It is good!" she said. "But it is small and thin. I fear it will break."

His mother went on. "Mateo, Grandmother is sick. I must take food to her. You have work to do while I am gone."

"Do you wish me to watch the fire?" Mateo asked.

"I could not fire the *ollas* this morning," his mother said. "You came too late with the wood. But it is just as well that there is no fire to watch, since I must go away."

"I will go with you to Grandmother's house," Mateo offered.

"No, son," his mother said. "Rafael is bringing some tourists to see how the black pottery is made. You and Concha must be ready to help."

Then she said, "You must sweep the patio and set out the chairs. Have the clay ready, too. Cover it well with a wet cloth."

Mateo nodded.

"Put out a large *olla,* one that is almost dry. When I come back, I will finish it as the tourists watch.

"I will go now," Mama said. "*Adiós!* Till we meet again!" She started down the road.

"*Adiós,* Mama!" Mateo answered.

After Mama had gone, Mateo sat on the ground. How his fingers wanted to make another clay horse, one that would help him remember Panchita! If only there were time to do it now! But he must do as his mother said. Mateo and Concha got everything ready for the tourists.

Soon there was the sound of cars in the road. Car doors slammed. People were talking. Rafael and the tourists walked onto the patio.

Mateo ran to Rafael and drew him aside. "All is ready," he whispered, "but Mama is not here. This morning she went to Grandmother's house, and she has not come back."

"Don't worry," Rafael said. "I will show the kiln and the clay, and the clay things your mother has made. She will come before long."

Mateo stood near the table where the tourists were looking at the small toys. He did not understand their words, but he could tell that they liked the fine work. He was proud. He and Concha had made these toys. If the little clay horse were here on the table, Mateo wondered, would they like it, too?

Rafael was talking to the tourists. "We will go to see the kiln where the pottery is fired. Only the potters of this village know the secret of making it black."

Now the time had come when Mama would make an *olla.* But Mama was not there!

Some of the tourists were standing up and moving about the patio. Soon they would go away. They would not see how the black pottery was made.

If only Mama would come, Mateo thought.

He stood up and ran quickly out to the road again.

191

Someone was walking down the road. But it was not Mama. It was Big Pablo leading Panchita away from the village!

Mateo sighed. "*Adiós,* Panchita," he said sadly.

Mateo went back to the tourists. If only he could make an *olla* for them to see. But Mama had said that he was too small to work with the large jars. If he made a little toy whistle no one would be able to see it.

He could make a horse like the beautiful Panchita! Today Mama had said that his little horse was good. Should he make a larger one while the people watched?

Suddenly, Mateo sat down and picked up a lump of the wet clay. He shaped the round body, small head, and tiny ears.

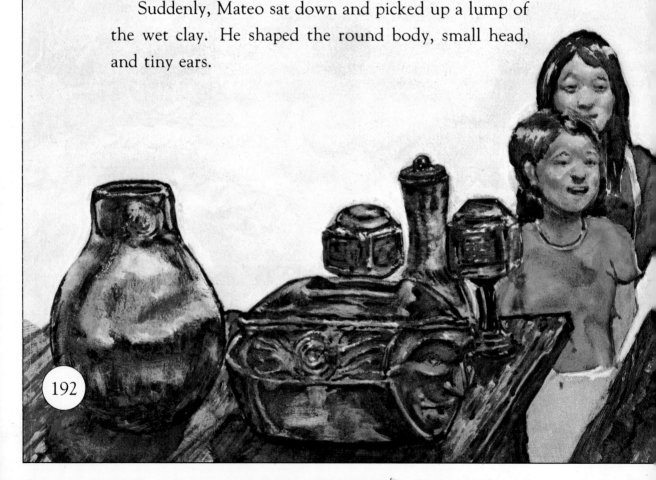

The people began to watch him work.

He made the arched neck with the mane flying in the wind. With rolls of clay he formed the legs. Another roll made the tail, which he flattened with a wet finger. The little horse was starting to look just like Panchita.

Smiling proudly, Mateo held up his work. The people watching smiled back. Looking beyond them, Mateo saw his mother. She had been watching as he made the clay horse!

Mateo felt his fingers grow stiff. He wanted to drop the horse and run away. His mother was one of the finest potters in all of Mexico. He could not work as she watched. It was his mother who should be showing the tourists how to work the clay.

Putting the horse down, Mateo asked his mother to come and take his place. She shook her head.

Mateo picked up the little horse. Mama wanted him to finish! He could not believe it! But she was smiling and waiting for him to go on.

He took up a sharp stick and drew the eyes. He made the fine lines on the mane and tail to look like hair. He wet his fingers in the bowl of water. Then he smoothed over the little body. He was finished.

He looked up at his mother.

She came forward, and Mateo said quickly, "I could not make an *olla* like yours, Mama. So I made a big horse like Panchita."

She took the clay horse from him. She turned it over carefully. "It is well made, little son," she said. "It will fire well."

Those were the finest words Mama could say. A

rush of happiness flooded over Mateo.

The people had left their chairs. They were crowding around and talking to Rafael.

"Many would like to buy the horse when it is fired," Rafael said to Mateo. "Will you make others?"

"I do not know," Mateo said, looking at his mother. She smiled at him and nodded.

"*Sí!*" Mateo said proudly. "I will make many more."

Yes, he thought, he would make more horses like the lovely Panchita, and he would always remember her. He would learn to make beautiful things that had never been made before. He would become one of the fine potters of the village.

Focus

1. What did Mateo want to make from clay? Why did he make it?

2. What did Mateo's mother think of the first horse he made?

3. How did Mateo feel when his mother looked at the second horse he made?

4. Sometimes people are dreamers. Sometimes they are doers. Which do you think Mateo was? Give reasons for your answer.

Mateo loved one horse so much that he made a clay horse just like her. Other people have loved horses. And they have found many ways to use horses.

HORSES

MARY EMERSON

Thousands of years ago many people lived in caves. They hunted their food on foot. Sometimes the food they hunted was horses. But they liked horses, too. They drew pictures of them on the walls of caves.

Later, people began to catch horses. They found that horses were easy to train. Horses were no longer hunted for food. They were used to help the people hunt. A horse could run much faster than a person could.

After hundreds of years, people began raising horses for special reasons. Some were bred to be fast, to carry messengers. Some were bred to be strong. They could pull plows or heavy wagons.

Today people still breed and train horses and ponies. Quarter horses are trained to be cow ponies. Morgans are often trained to be police horses.

How do you train horses? First, the horse must want to work for you. Be generous with your praise. Be firm, but patient and kind. Also, start training a horse when it is young. Show the horse that people are friendly.

Are these new ideas? No! More than a thousand years ago a Greek trainer wrote about ways to train horses. Many years later an English trainer found that a horse can remember what it is taught. That trainer said that you should repeat each lesson many times. Then the horse will learn it.

Circus horses are trained this way. In fact, the first circus horses were trained to do more than one thing. Each circus used horses to pull the wagons from one town to the next. Once the tent was set up, the same horses were part of the show!

There are two main kinds of circus horses. One is called the Liberty horse. Liberty horses are trained to gallop around a ring. They work in teams of eight or sixteen. They can start or stop quickly, and walk on their back legs.

The horses that bareback riders use are called Rosinbacks. They got that name because their backs are rubbed with rosin before each show. Rosin is a sticky gum. It keeps the riders from slipping. A Rosinback must move very smoothly. It must not get scared by the other acts. It must not get excited by the music or the crowd. If it gets excited, its rider could fall.

It takes many years to train a Rosinback. The trainer stands in the center of the ring. Each new trick is taught with care. All the while the trainer gives the horse a lot of praise.

A Rosinback and its rider are close friends. A bareback rider will use only one horse. Sometimes the horse gets sick or too old to work. Then the rider has to start all over with a new horse and new tricks.

Horses are not used as much today as they once were. But, like the people who painted pictures of horses on the walls of caves, people still love horses.

Focus

1. Tell three ways people have used horses over the years.
2. What is the first step in training a horse?
3. What is a Liberty horse? What is a Rosinback?
4. What is the main idea of this story?

Many stories use words that may be new to you. Mateo put a *mane* on his clay horse. If you don't know what a *mane* is, how can you find out?

Suppose you read that a horse pulls on its *bit.* You know that *bit* is almost like *bite.* But that meaning does not make sense in the story. How could you find the other meaning for the word *bit?* You could look up *bit* in a dictionary.

There are two words at the top of a dictionary page. They are called *guide words.* The first guide word tells the first word on that page. The second guide word tells the last word on that page.

Look at the next page. It has part of a dictionary of words about horses. Study the dictionary page. Then answer these questions on your paper.

1. How does a dictionary help you? What does it tell you?
2. What meaning of the word *hand* is given?
3. What is the difference between a colt and a filly?
4. Where would you find a frog on a horse?
5. There are three meanings given for the word *bridle.* What are they?

bit (bit) *noun.* the part of a bridle that fits in a horse's mouth.

bri·dle (brī'dl) *noun.* headgear used to control the horse. —*verb.* 1. to put a bridle on. 2. to restrain.

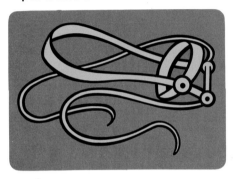

bronc (brongk) *noun.* a wild, untamed horse.

can·ter (kan'tər) *noun.* a horse's easy gallop.

colt (kōlt) *noun.* a male horse less than four years old.

fil·ly (fil'ē) *noun.* a female horse less than four years old.

foal (fōl) *noun.* a horse less than one year old. —*verb.* to give birth to a foal.

frog (frôg) *noun.* part of a horse's hoof.

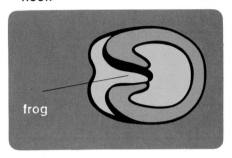

frog

gait (gāt) *noun.* the way a horse moves; its gait may be a walk, trot, canter, or gallop.

gal·lop (gal'əp) *noun.* the fastest gait of a horse. —*verb.* to go or cause to go at a gallop.

groom (grüm) *verb.* to clean and take care of a horse.

hal·ter (hôl'tər) *noun.* the rope or strap for leading or tying a horse.

hand (hand) *noun.* a unit to measure a horse's height; one hand is equal to four inches.

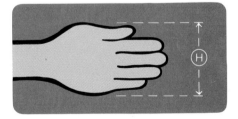

hock (hok) *noun.* the joint on the hind leg of a horse.

hoof (hůf) *noun.* the foot of a horse.

201

Mateo loved horses, and so does Caroline. In this story a horse surprises Caroline and is the solution to a problem.

DREAM
DANCER

EVELYN BOLTON

Every year Caroline comes to Santa D'Oro to stay with her grandfather. Her grandfather works at Mr. Judd's Hand-Crafted Furniture Factory.

Mr. Judd is an important man in Santa D'Oro. He owns the hotel and the big riding stables. He also owns the house where Caroline's grandfather lives.

Caroline works in Mr. Judd's stables during the summer. In return, Mr. Judd lets her pick the horse she wants to ride in the big Fourth of July parade. Caroline always picked Dandy until . . .

Caroline's bus turned into the town square and stopped. She saw her grandfather under the big tree on the corner.

"Grandpa! Grandpa! I'm back!" Caroline called.

She was off the bus. Her grandpa was hugging her.

"Let me look at you." He held her at arm's length. "You are taller and stronger, and getting to look more like me every day."

"Oh, Grandpa!" Caroline laughed. He'd said the same thing last year, and the year before, too.

They sat on the porch, rocking in the small handmade rockers. Her grandpa had made those rockers, and he was proud of them. Grandpa would tell anyone about his work. "Our furniture is all handmade. We make fine things here!"

"How is Dandy, Grandpa?"

"As far as I know, he's fine. Mr. Judd says you can get him first thing in the morning."

Caroline felt so warm and happy that she closed her eyes. Her grandpa touched her leg with his foot.

"You're worn out, and the big parade is tomorrow. You'd best get on up to bed."

Caroline was tired. Without another word she went up to her bedroom. She was almost asleep when her grandpa came in.

"Good night," he said softly. He waited as though wanting to say more. There was a feeling in the room that made her afraid.

"Is something wrong?" Caroline asked.

"Nothing is wrong. Sleep well."

She did sleep well. It seemed only five minutes later when she opened her eyes. Her grandfather came in, carrying the smooth, handmade tray. On it were milk and toast and an egg in her own egg cup.

"First-morning treat," he said. Caroline sat up and rubbed her eyes. It was the Fourth of July! It was Dandy Day!

Her grandpa sat on the edge of the bed. "I want to tell you something. . . . Well, I really don't want to tell you, least of all today. But if I don't tell you, somebody else might."

Caroline waited. Something in his voice made her feel odd. Grandpa said, "After next week I won't be working for Mr. Judd any more. I have to retire."

What? Her grandfather not working? He never even took a day off, except holidays. Grandpa was always at his bench in Mr. Judd's furniture shop.

"But Grandpa, why do you have to retire?"

He tried a smile. "I'll be seventy years old. That's the way it's done."

"But that doesn't make sense!" Anger was rising in her, hot and hurting. "Everyone knows you're the best furniture maker in Santa D'Oro . . . in California . . . in the country! So what does being seventy have to do with it?"

She picked up the wooden egg cup carved with

leaves and flowers. At least Grandpa would not have to sit in his rocker all day, doing nothing. He'd still be able to make things in his shop out back. . . . "Will you be able to stay on here, in Mr. Judd's house?" she asked.

His eyes slid from hers. "Well, maybe I'll take a room somewhere. But let's not talk about it now."

"But . . ."

"Time to get up, Caroline. It's time for the parade, and Dandy's waiting."

Caroline lay back. "I don't want Mr. Judd's horse," she said. "I'm not going!" She was furious.

Her grandpa stood up. "You are going. Mr. Judd has always been kind to us, and he's probably right."

"But Grandpa! Did you ask if you could keep on working? If you asked . . ."

"No! That's the way it's always been done at Judd's, and a person can't beg."

Caroline sat straight. "I know! I'll ask him. He likes me. He calls me his City Girl."

"Caroline!" She couldn't remember ever hearing him use that voice before. "You'll say nothing! Do you understand me? Nothing!" She knew there was no use arguing.

Caroline dressed quickly, ran downstairs and outside. Grandpa was waiting for her.

"I'll be in my usual place under the bank sign," he said. "You be sure to wave to me."

Caroline nodded. She watched as he turned toward Main Street. Suddenly it seemed that Grandpa looked older than last year.

"Don't think about it now," she told herself.

"Think about Dandy. Dandy!"

Mr. Judd's stable hand, Charlie, came out of the office. He smiled at her. "Hi, Caroline! It's good to see you!"

"Hi, Charlie. I've come for Dandy."

"He's back by the barn. I figured you would be in a hurry, so he's groomed and blanketed already. I'll be there in a minute to help you saddle up."

"Thanks." Caroline could see Dandy waiting for her. Dandy! She began to run.

"Say!" Charlie called after her. "Are you sure you want Dandy? We've got another good-looking horse

you could take instead."

"No!" Caroline shook her head. She ran along the path to the barn and stepped inside the gate. Dandy's ears lifted.

"You remember me, don't you?" Caroline whispered. She rubbed his soft nose.

An old gray stood nearby. His ears sagged. His legs were thick, heavily feathered below the knees. Caroline slipped through the fence and walked toward the gray.

"I guess they think you're too old for a parade," Caroline said softly. "There's probably some kind of rule about it." Caroline felt a pity for the old horse that was half anger.

Suddenly Caroline knew what she had to do. She slipped through the fence again and ran to the barn. The box of grooming tools was in its usual place. She carried it back to the old gray. She brushed him, working hard and fast. The parade was about to start and she didn't have much time.

Charlie came up the path. "What are you doing? You're not going to ride him, are you?"

"Yes I am!" She took the saddle blanket from Charlie. "And I'm running out of time. Hurry!"

"Look, Caroline. Mr. Judd is not going to want that old horse in his parade."

"His parade!" Caroline said.

"Please take Dandy, the way you always do."

Caroline pulled at the saddle. "If you won't saddle him, I'll do it myself!"

"OK! OK!" Charlie tossed the saddle on the gray's back. "Wait till the boss sees you. He got this horse for new riders who need something slow. You're going to feel pretty silly if this horse won't walk for you. What if he falls down?"

Caroline didn't answer. She rode the gray out onto the dirt road.

"You know his name? Dream Dancer!" Charlie roared with laughter.

Caroline bent over the big gray's neck. "Come on, Dancer, come on. You've got to keep your head up! Walk a little faster . . . please . . . please?" Her hands were slippery on the reins. What if he did fall down? What would she do?

The parade started in the high school field. The gray didn't want to go among the people and horses. Caroline had to tap him with her heels.

Mr. Judd was in the middle of everything, riding his beautiful horse, Spring Boy. "His parade," Caroline thought, "and his factory and his town!"

Mr. Judd was moving everyone into place. "I want the color guard first," he said. "You get by the gate. The Santa D'Oro band comes next. You rodeo stars come after the band." Mr. Judd saw Caroline.

"Hi, City Girl!" He looked down. "Where's Dandy?"

"I took the gray instead." Caroline kept her eyes on Mr. Judd. "He doesn't want to stand around all day when other horses are busy. Just because he's seventy years old."

Mr. Judd looked at her. "Caroline! Your grandpa told you!"

"My grandpa told me not to talk to you about him, so I can't," Caroline said.

The color guard started marching, and the Santa

D'Oro band began to play. Caroline saw Dancer's ears move forward. He trembled. She bent forward to whisper in his ear.

"Please, Dancer. Please! Don't give up on me. We haven't started yet!" Dream Dancer trembled again.

"He's going to fall!" Caroline thought. She held on with her knees and edged him into line. The parade moved out onto the road.

Now the music picked up. There was the high, clean sound of the trumpets and the growl of the tuba.

Something was wrong with Dancer! He pulled at the bit, arching his neck like a horse on show. . . .

Caroline called to the rider next to her. "Tim! Tim! Look at Dancer!"

Dream Dancer was dancing and prancing to the music. His big legs lifted gracefully. His white mane tossed to the bobbing of his head. He began to move in and out, now in front of Tim's horse, now behind him.

"Mr. Judd!" Tim called. "Come and look at Caroline's stylish horse."

Mr. Judd looked at Dancer. "Well!" he said. "That old horse trader said Dream Dancer used to be a circus horse. I guess Dancer remembers the music."

"I guess so," Caroline said. She held the reins free.

"Bring Dancer up front, behind the color guard," Mr. Judd said. "We don't want anyone to miss this."

Caroline wheeled her dancing, prancing horse into the place of honor. "I guess he doesn't know he's

supposed to be seventy," she said.

"You're talking about your grandpa again," Mr. Judd warned. But his voice was soft.

"No, sir!" Caroline said. "Grandpa said not to talk about him, and I can't."

The roar of the crowd was all around them. Dream Dancer stepped even higher to the sound of the cheers.

"He could give summer shows for the children, Mr. Judd," Caroline said. "It would be too bad to waste him."

Mr. Judd smiled. "If there's one thing I can't stand, it's waste," he said. "I guess I've got some thinking to do . . . about the old horse, I mean. After all, we can't

talk about your grandpa. You've told me that a dozen times."

Caroline looked up at him. There was so much understanding on Mr. Judd's face that she knew everything was going to be all right.

Focus

1. What did Grandpa tell Caroline at breakfast on the Fourth of July?
2. Why did Caroline choose to ride the old gray instead of Dandy?
3. How did Dream Dancer surprise the people at the parade?
4. What do you think Mr. Judd will do about Grandpa's job? Why?

CHECKPOINT

Read the paragraph below. From the list, choose the word that best fits each sentence. Number your paper from 1–5. Write the correct word beside the number.

patio   saddle   mane   whistle
circus   groomed   Caroline   retired

(**1**) _____ loved horses. Her horse was named Star. Star always came when Caroline blew her (**2**) _____. Every day Caroline took a brush and (**3**) _____ Star. She combed Star's (**4**) _____. Then she would put a (**5**) _____ on Star's back. Caroline took good care of Star.

Read the paragraph. Then answer the questions. Write the answers on your paper.

Marco's sister, Blanca, is a horse trainer. Her horses have won many prizes. Marco has a picture of Blanca on his bedroom wall. It shows Blanca with her favorite horse. The horse is wearing a blue ribbon and Blanca is smiling. Marco wants to be a horse trainer, too. He hopes Blanca will teach him.

6. Which sentence is most likely true?
   a. Marco wishes his sister were a banker.
   b. Marco thinks Blanca is foolish to care about horses.
   c. Marco is proud of his sister.

7. Which sentence is most likely true?

    a. Blanca is a good horse trainer.

    b. Blanca does not really like her job.

    c. Blanca would rather be a pilot.

Read the sentences below. Choose the word that best completes each sentence. Write the words on your paper.

Decoding:
Suffixes *-ish, -ous*

  8. He was being very silly and acting (clown; clownish).

  9. What a (marvel; marvelous) the human body is!

10. If something is unsafe, it is (danger; dangerous).

Read the dictionary entry below. Then answer the questions that follow. Write the answers on your paper.

Study Skills:
Dictionary

hand (hand) *noun.* 1. the end of the arm: Each *hand* has four fingers and a thumb. 2. a worker who uses his hands. 3. the unit to measure a horse's height. —*verb.* to give with the hand: Please *hand* me that bowl.

11. How many meanings does the word *hand* have?

12. Which meaning has to do with horses?

13. Which meaning would fit this sentence? "Charlie is Mr. Judd's stable hand."

217

Dar

Doing something for the first time is not always easy. It can even be scary. Sometimes the hardest part is just daring to try. These stories tell about doing something for the first time. Eva is alone in an ice cave. Linda is called on to help a sick child. Each person dares. Each succeeds in his or her own way.

Sometimes people need to find a new way to do things. That can be scary, too. Some folks need a new way to make gingerbread. Others work at outwitting a nasty dragon. You will find some new ways in these stories.

ing

to Try

Everybody lives special moments. For Eva it is her first
walk alone on the bottom of the sea.

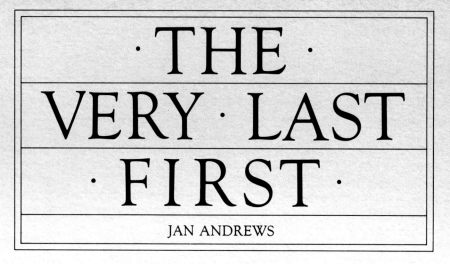

· THE ·
VERY · LAST
· FIRST ·

JAN ANDREWS

Eva Padlyat lives in a village on Ungava Bay. It is in
the north of Quebec, in Canada. She's Inuit, and for as
long as she can remember, she's known how to walk on

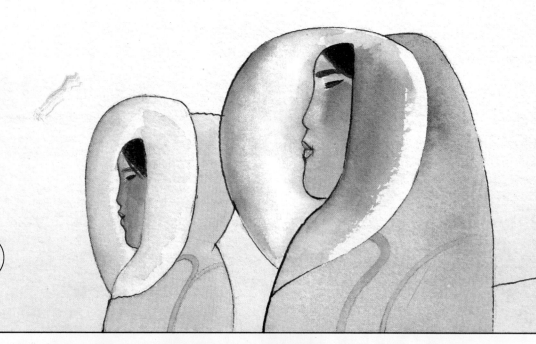

the bottom of the sea. It's something the people of her village often do, in winter, when they want mussels to eat. Today, though, something special is going to happen. Today, for the very first time in her life, Eva will walk on the bottom of the sea alone.

Eva and her mother stand in the small, warm kitchen of their home. They put on heavy parkas and go out. They pull their hoods close to protect their faces from the cold wind and the sting of whipped-up snow. It is January, one of the worst months in the long Ungava winter.

Eva and her mother walk through the village. Each pulls behind her a small sled. On the sleds are a shovel, a long ice chisel, and a pan for mussels. Snow lies white as far as the eye can see. There are no trees for miles and miles on the vast northern tundra. There are no highways, either. The village is off and away by itself.

The street Eva and her mother are on takes them past the school and down to the seashore. They meet a few friends on the way and stop for a quick greeting.

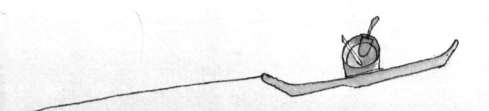

Then they go on to cross the snow-covered beach. They step out on the thick sea ice. They've come at just the right time. The tide has pulled back from the land, and there won't be any water near the shore. They can go under the ice and wander about on the sea bed quite safely.

"Good-by," Eva's mother says. "Be careful, and good luck."

Eva grins. "Good luck, yourself," she replies.

Eva plods on over bumps and ridges where the cold has frozen the waves. She looks toward the open sea beyond the bay. She sees only ice and more ice, on and on. Finally, Eva stops in what seems to be a good place, where the ice is raised and swollen. She shovels away a patch of snow. Then she works the sharp end of her chisel under a heaved-up crack in the ice to make a hole. It's hard work. The freeze-up came months ago, and the ice is very thick.

When the hole is about two feet square, Eva lowers herself into the darkness. She stands in the under-ice cavern—proud and excited and alone. Eva lights a candle and watches the yellow light soften the blackness. The small light glistens on the ice shining over her head. It shines on the wet, black stones and pools and seaweed at her feet.

Then, for a moment, she's afraid. It's too dark to see far. She knows it can be dangerous down here. The under-ice world stretches far across the bay. Out there the sea tide is already beginning to lap back. She'll have to be careful. If she forgets how long she's been down, the tide could catch her. If she goes too far, she could lose her way back. Eva shivers, then laughs to herself.

"I'd better get to work," she says.

Eva puts her candle between two stones and starts collecting mussels. She has chosen her spot well. Wherever she turns, her candle shows up strings of blue-black mussel shells. Before long, her pan is full.

Eva goes back to the ice hole. She sets her pan down and listens for the sound of the waves. The tide is still quite a way out. There's plenty of time to do what she has always wanted. Now she can enjoy being by herself down here in the dark, mysterious, undersea winter world.

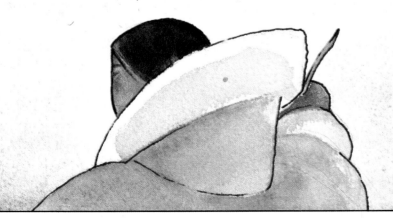

Eva sings a tune, quietly at first, then loudly. The echoes of her singing bounce off the ice at her. She shouts to herself and is glad. She dances a little dance. She pokes in rock pools and makes strange shadows with her candle. She lifts up seaweed in long, flat ribbon strands. Then she lets them down with a flop.

At last Eva hears a voice. Her mother is calling through the ice hole. "Are you all right down there? Are you nearly done?"

Eva takes her candle, and goes back to the hole. She

picks up her mussel pan. "Of course I'm all right. I'm coming up now."

She climbs out into the fresh air and feels the cold wind on her face again.

"You've done well," her mother says. "You must have chosen a better place than I did."

They load up the sleds again, and Eva takes her mother's hand. Together they walk over the ice. They cross the beach and go through the village. Already, twilight has fallen. Daylight lasts a very few hours this far north in January.

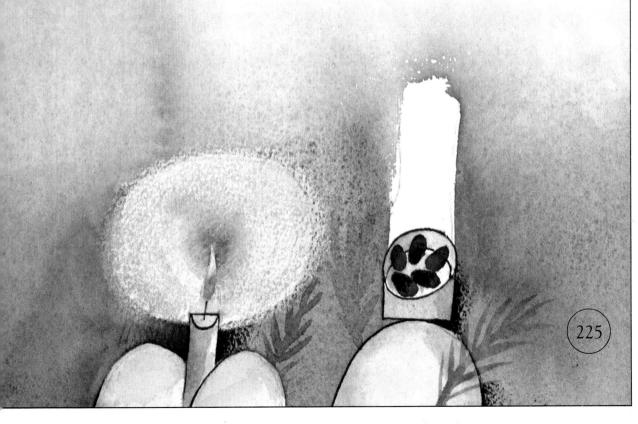

Eva glances back over her shoulder at the mussel shells. She thinks of popping them in boiling water, watching them open, and tasting the salty fish in her mouth.

"That's my last very first time," she says sadly. "My very last very first time for walking alone under the sea."

Eva's mother laughs. "You really like it down there, don't you?"

"Yes," Eva answers. "Yes, I do." She thinks of the black glistening ice and the faint humming of the tide far out to sea. She remembers being frightened when she first stood alone in the huge cavern. She remembers dancing on the sea floor once her mussel pan was full. Eva looks back toward the bay, then up at her mother. "I like it down there. It's fun."

Focus

1. Why did the people of Eva's village walk on the bottom of the sea?
2. What was special about Eva's walk?
3. Eva knew that walking under the ice could be dangerous. Name two things that Eva had to watch out for.
4. Eva was sad when her walk ended. What made her sad?

Eva had a moment of fear under the ice. When Linda is asked to help a sick boy, she is frightened, too. Will she remember what to do?

LINDA RICHARDS

DAVID R. COLLINS

Linda Richards was the first nurse who was trained in America. When Linda was quite young, her father died. Then her mother got very sick. Doc Currier, the family's doctor, watched Linda tend to her mother. He saw that she was very good at making her mother comfortable.

After Linda's mother died, Linda moved in with Grandma and Grandpa Sinclair. Her greatest wish was to learn how to care for the sick.

Linda liked to help Grandpa with the farm animals. Soon all the animals seemed like friends to her. Linda talked to them and called them by name. When she gathered the eggs, the hens clucked to her. Her pet rooster followed her all over the farm.

Grandpa always knew where to find Linda.

227

One corner of the barn was special to her. There she cared for her animal "patients."

"If I get sick, will you take good care of me like that?" Grandpa teased her as he watched Linda spoon-feed a baby rabbit.

Doc Currier stopped by when he could. He liked to watch Linda work with the animals. "You've got a good barnyard hospital here," he laughed. "I wouldn't

mind being a sick cow on this farm."

"You're just like Grandpa," Linda said. "I'm glad my animal patients don't tease me all the time."

Other people heard about Linda's barnyard hospital. Soon she was caring for pet dogs, pet cats, and even a pet goat.

Then, on her thirteenth birthday, Linda got a surprise present. Doc Currier asked her to go with him on some sick calls. Doc had remembered her wish! Linda scrambled up into the buggy, eager to get started.

Doc Currier often came to pick up his new helper. Sometimes they left the house at sunrise and did not return until dark. As the buggy bumped along the dirt roads, Linda asked questions. "What is the best way to stop bleeding? How can you tell if a bone is really broken?"

Doc Currier answered each question carefully. He knew Linda would try to remember every word he said.

At first Linda helped only with the small jobs. She boiled water and ripped bandage cloths. By the time a year had passed, Doc Currier had taught her a lot. He showed her how to clean wounds, put on bandages, and set splints on broken bones.

"Treating sick people calls for calm and careful thinking," Doc Currier told Linda. "Decide what needs to be done and do it. Sometimes you'll feel frightened. Just don't let your fear show. Stay calm. Your patient must trust you and have faith in you. Don't forget that."

One cold night a strange buggy stopped in front of Grandpa's house. The driver leaped up the porch steps. He pounded on the door.

"We can't find Doc Currier," the young man told Grandpa. "My wife said to come here and bring back the Richards girl. My boy's sick—real sick."

Linda heard the man. Before Grandpa could call she had put on her coat. Soon she hurried through the door of a tiny white house. In the bedroom a woman sat beside a young boy.

"Oh, I'm so glad you've come! Tommy's so hot. He won't open his eyes. I don't know what to do."

Linda barely heard her words. She saw that Tommy's skin was dry. The boy was restless under the heavy quilt. Linda tried to remember everything Doc Currier had told her about fever. She had never taken care of a patient without him. She was frightened, but there was no time to lose.

"We've got to break this fever," Linda said. "We'll need chipped ice and towels."

Tommy's father hurried out into the snowy yard to hunt for chunks of ice. The boy's mother and Linda got the towels ready. Linda filled a towel with ice chips. Then she stroked Tommy's head and chest with the cool, damp cloth.

Hour after hour Linda went on with the ice baths. By morning her own body was tired and aching. But Tommy seemed cooler and more comfortable.

At last Doc Currier came. Linda ran to the door to meet him. "I tried not to be afraid," she whispered in Doc's ear. "But I was—at first."

Slowly Doc Currier examined Tommy. He asked Linda a few questions. Finally the old man stood up.

"Tommy is going to be just fine," he said. "He's a strong boy, and he's had a good nurse here. She did everything for him I could have done."

Linda felt happy at Doc's words. She knew she would never again be afraid to treat a patient.

Focus

1. On her thirteenth birthday, Linda got a surprise present. What was the present?

2. Did it take courage for Linda to take care of Tommy? Write down the sentences that show how she felt.

3. Doc Currier gave Linda good advice about treating sick people. How did his advice help her?

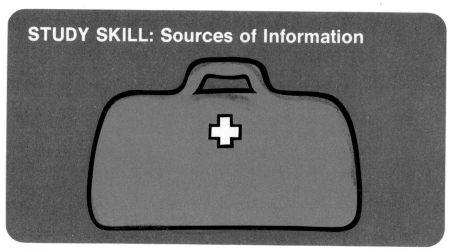

STUDY SKILL: Sources of Information

You just read a story about Linda Richards. Stories can tell you about people like Linda. Other kinds of writing can give you facts about people, too.

We often get facts from more than one source, or book. It is a good idea to read different sources. Each source gives you more and different ideas.

Read the two passages below. Both are about Elizabeth Blackwell. Each gives a different kind of information.

1. Blackwell, Elizabeth (1821–1910), the first woman doctor in the United States. Born in England, she came to the United States at the age of 10. In 1849 she graduated from the Geneva, New York, College of Medicine. In 1853 she opened a hospital for women and children in New York City. In 1857 she founded the Women's Medical College. Elizabeth Blackwell became a well-known doctor in this country and in England. In 1869 she moved back to England. She became a professor of medicine at the London School of Medicine.

2. "Elizabeth never lost sight of her goal. While teaching school, she studied medicine on the side. Doctors who were friendly to her cause taught her what they could. She was finally allowed to study medicine. The male students did not like having a woman in their classes. They made life difficult for Elizabeth. Still, she kept on and became a doctor. She was also first in her class!"

Answer the questions. First, number your paper 1 to 5. Next to each number, write the number of the passage that is the answer to that question.

1. Which passage tells that Blackwell became a doctor?
2. Which passage tells that Blackwell always wanted to be a doctor?
3. Which passage tells how some doctors treated Blackwell?
4. Which passage tells the most facts about Blackwell's life?
5. Which fact is in both passages?

    a. Blackwell was first in her class.

    b. Blackwell was a doctor.

    c. Blackwell was a professor of medicine.

Linda was courageous to help Tommy. Mary Jo needs courage, too, when she is alone with her grandmother on the farm.

Mary Jo's Grandmother

JANICE MAY UDRY

The leaves began to fall from the trees and the days grew colder. Mary Jo's mother and father began to worry. They tried to get Grandmother to move into town.

"You haven't even got a telephone. You shouldn't be living all alone way out here," Mary Jo's mother fretted. "Why, your nearest neighbor is clear beyond the main road."

Grandmother smiled. "Now don't you worry about me. I'm all prepared for winter. I'm as snug as can be here. Don't you fret about me."

Sometimes Mary Jo's sister had stayed by herself for a few days with Grandmother. And sometimes Jeff had stayed out there, too. This year, for the first time, Mary Jo was going to stay on by herself during part of

Thanksgiving vacation.

The family always went to Grandmother's for Thanksgiving dinner. It was all they could do to squeeze together around Grandmother's table.

It was a happy family day. Everybody was talking, singing, laughing, and teasing.

In the evening, Grandmother and Mary Jo waved good-by to everybody from the porch. After the last car went down the drive in the dusk, it was very quiet.

Grandmother gazed out over the bare trees at the sky. "Snow tonight," she said.

After supper and a piece of sweet potato pie for each of them, Grandmother turned out the lights. ("You always go to bed very early at Grandmother's," Jeff had told Mary Jo.) Just before she fell asleep, Mary Jo saw great flakes of snow, like feathers, falling outside the little square window.

Mary Jo woke early the next morning. She could already hear Grandmother in the kitchen.

"Beautiful snow, beautiful snow," sang Mary Jo when she looked out the window. The countryside was filled with purest white, and the snow was still falling.

"This is the most snow I ever saw here this early in the winter," said Grandmother. "Here, Mary Jo, take these bread crumbs out to the birds while I get some jam from the back pantry."

Mary Jo had to sweep snow ahead of herself so she could walk out on the porch. She swept one corner of the porch and put out the crumbs. Before she was back inside the door, hungry birds were fluttering over them.

Grandmother had not come back from the pantry yet. It was a smallish room built two steps down at the back of the house. It was cool and dark.

Then, from the open pantry door, Mary Jo heard a moan. Her grandmother called weakly, "Mary Jo!"

"What happened?" said Mary Jo running to the door. She looked down. Her grandmother was lying on the pantry floor. She had tripped and fallen down the steps!

"I can't get up," moaned Grandmother.

"I'm coming! I'll help you," said Mary Jo.

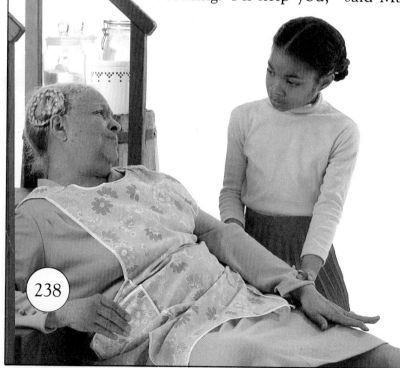

She hurried to the pantry. Mary Jo knelt beside her grandmother and tried to lift her. Grandmother winced with pain.

"No, Mary Jo, don't try to lift me. I think my ankle is sprained. Maybe my leg is broken," she said. "Now I'm in a fine fix!"

Mary Jo wondered how on earth she could move her grandmother.

"It's my left leg. It hurts too much to move it."

"Don't worry, Grandmother," said Mary Jo. She looked around at the dark little pantry. It was not very warm. Mary Jo ran back through the kitchen. She went into a bedroom. She pulled blankets and a pillow off the bed. She took them to the pantry and wrapped the blankets around her grandmother. Then she carefully put the pillow under her head.

"Oh, good girl," said her grandmother. "Thank goodness you are here, Mary Jo. Just let me rest while I think of what to do. I'll be all right. You go and have some breakfast."

Grandmother leaned her head back and closed her eyes.

Mary Jo went to the kitchen and poured some coffee into a cup. She took it out to her grandmother. She gently lifted her head so that she could sip the hot coffee.

239

"Ah, that's good!" said her grandmother gratefully.

Mary Jo went back into the kitchen and looked out the window at the deepening snow. "I don't even have my boots here," she thought.

She knew that she must go for help. There was no neighbor next door to call. She must walk to the main road because Grandmother had no telephone. No one would be passing by on the little road where her grandmother lived.

She went back into the pantry. Grandmother opened her eyes.

"Grandmother, I'm going up to the main road for help," said Mary Jo.

"In all this snow?" said her grandmother.

"I can do it," said Mary Jo.

Her grandmother sighed and leaned her head back on the pillow again. "I guess I'll have to let you go, Mary Jo," she said. "Wrap up good and warm."

"Yes, Grandmother," said Mary Jo. "You rest and don't worry."

"I'll be all right. I'm a tough old bird," murmured her grandmother.

Mary Jo found a pair of old boots in a closet. She made them fit by stuffing the toes full of newspaper. She put on two sweaters, a coat, and an old stocking cap.

Mary Jo went to ask her grandmother if she needed anything. Grandmother appeared to be asleep. Or had she fainted?

Mary Jo hurried out into the snow, making sure the back door was closed.

The snow had stopped falling, but icy wind tossed handfuls of it around the corner of the house and into her face. Mary Jo walked as fast as she could down the

long drive. How she wished there were a neighbor close by!

It took her twice as long as it usually did just to reach the old mailbox. The snow in the road was untouched. No truck or car had been along.

Mary Jo trudged toward the main road, lifting her feet high at each step in the old heavy boots. She had never felt so much alone as she did in that cold, windy, white world. She never even saw a squirrel.

Mary Jo finally reached the main highway. She could see that no cars had been along there, either. The snow was too deep. Mary Jo's legs had never felt so tired before.

She had to rest before starting to walk to the nearest house.

Then up the road she saw a black speck moving slowly closer. She stared at it. Then she waved.

"It's the snowplow!" she cried. Although no one was there, she wanted to hear the words herself because she was so glad.

It seemed to take forever for the machine to reach Mary Jo. Finally the men saw her and waved. Mary Jo jumped up and down to keep warm.

The driver stopped the snowplow and leaned over. "What are you doing out here?"

Mary Jo explained to him what had happened.

"Can you call my father in town? His name is William Wood."

"Sure!" said the man. "But what about you? You can't walk all the way back in this."

"I must get back to my grandmother," said Mary Jo.

"Did you ever ride on a snowplow?"

Mary Jo shook her head.

"Here, climb up. We'll clear the road down to your grandmother's and let you off there. Then we'll go on to the next house and phone your father."

"It's a good thing you were at the corner," said the driver. "We wouldn't have cleared this side road until tomorrow. We clear out only the main roads the first day after a big snow like this."

Mary Jo got off at her grandmother's drive. She waved good-by and walked back up to the house. The men on the snowplow said that they would telephone her father from the first house.

When Mary Jo went into the pantry, her grandmother's eyes were open. She smiled. "How did you get back so fast, child?"

Mary Jo told her about the snowplow. "Mother and Dad will be here in a little while," she said. "All our worries are over now, Grandmother. I'll go heat some soup."

"That sounds good," said Grandmother. "I'm

feeling better already. Thank goodness you were here, Mary Jo."

Mary Jo went into the kitchen. She prepared a nice lunch. Then she and her grandmother ate it together in the pantry.

Soon after that, Mary Jo looked out the window.

Walking up the driveway she could see her mother and father and Jeff. They were just getting out of the car.

"They're here, Grandmother!" Mary Jo called, and ran to open the door.

Focus

1. Why were Mary Jo's parents so worried about Grandmother?
2. How did Mary Jo feel when she first saw the snow?
3. Mary Jo found her grandmother on the floor. What had happened?
4. When Grandmother got hurt, Mary Jo first tried to make her more comfortable. Tell what Mary Jo did.
5. We might say that Mary Jo showed a lot of courage. Tell one thing from the story that shows Mary Jo's courage.

CHECKPOINT

Vocabulary:
Word
Identification

Use the words below to fill in the blanks. On your paper write each sentence with the word that fits in it.

bay   hospital   shovel   mussels

buggy   blankets   pantry   pillow

1. When I broke my leg, I went to the _____.
2. The horse pulled the _____ down the street.
3. The hole was dug with a _____.
4. On cold nights I sleep with three _____.
5. The jars of fruit are kept in the _____.
6. The ship sailed into the _____.

Vocabulary:
Vocabulary
Development
(context clues)

Read the sentences that follow. Try to find out from the rest of the sentence what each underlined word means. Then write the answers on your paper.

It was <u>customary</u> for women in Eva's village to walk under the ice. They did it all the time.

7. What does the word <u>customary</u> mean?

usual   dressed up   rare

Linda learned how to be a nurse by <u>observing</u> the doctor. She watched everything he did.

8. What does the word <u>observing</u> mean?

bringing food to   liking   looking at

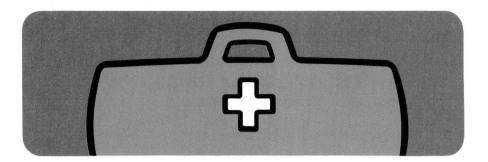

Choose the word that best completes each sentence.

Comprehension: Character

9. When Eva walked under the ice she felt _____.

excited   angry   social

10. When Doc called Linda a good nurse she felt _____.

angry   sad   proud

11. Mary Jo went to get help for her grandmother because Mary Jo was _____.

pleased   worried   angry

Complete each sentence with the best word. Write the sentences on your paper. Make up a sentence for the extra word.

Decoding: Long Words

compliment   amazed   determined   confidence

12. Eva had _____ in herself.

13. Linda was _____ to be a nurse.

14. Doc gave Linda a _____ when he said she was a good nurse.

247

Her grandmother relied on Mary Jo to get help.
King Pilaf wants a queen to bake his gingerbread.

The Queen Who Couldn't Bake Gingerbread

DOROTHY VAN WOERKOM

King Pilaf of Mulligatawny was having a very bad day. To begin with, he bumped his head against the Lord Chamberlain's. Then he discovered a hole in the heel of his stocking. And he knew without asking that his breakfast gingerbread would be crumbly again. He was miserable. He was lonely, too.

The king sat on the edge of his bed. He put his thumb through the hole in his stocking.

"It is time," he said, "that Mulligatawny had a queen and I a wife. She should be beautiful. That would please me. And she should be wise enough to help me rule."

The Lord Chamberlain slipped the king's stocking over the royal foot.

"A splendid idea, Your Majesty!" he said. "By happy chance I was thinking the very same thing myself. As a matter of fact . . ."

The king wagged his foot under the Lord Chamberlain's nose. He sighed loudly. "Don't give me one of your speeches so early in the day, my lord. Just help me into my boots. Then let's have some breakfast."

249

So they drank their lime juice and ate cheese omelet. The gingerbread crumbled. The king frowned at the crumbs on his plate. He said, "My queen should be more than just wise and beautiful. She should also know how to bake gingerbread."

Now it was the Lord Chamberlain who sighed. For when Pilaf had become king, he had turned Mulligatawny inside out to find a gingerbread baker.

"There isn't one in my kingdom who can bake it to a turn," the king was saying. "It should be neither too hard nor too soft. It must be just properly crisp."

Then the king called for their horses. Away they rode to the kingdom of Ghur. In Ghur there lived a princess as wise as she was beautiful. Her name was Madelon.

"No, I cannot bake gingerbread," Princess Madelon said. "But I make perfect little almond cakes."

King Pilaf thought about that: a queen both wise and beautiful, who could make pretty cakes. But at last he shook his head sadly.

"I'm sorry to say that it must be gingerbread," he said.

Then off he galloped with the Lord Chamberlain to the kingdom of Shoggen. Here lived a princess who was not as wise as she was beautiful. Her name was Jebelle.

"No, I cannot bake gingerbread," said Princess Jebelle. "But I can bake the best zwieback that you will ever taste."

Princess Jebelle would make a beautiful queen. But zwieback—no, the king could never like zwieback at all.

251

"I'm sorry to say that it must be gingerbread," he said.

King Pilaf kissed her hand. He rode away with his chamberlain to the kingdom of Tintinnabulum. Here lived a princess who was not as beautiful as she was wise. Her name was Calliope.

"Ah, King Pilaf!" Princess Calliope cried. "You are, I suppose, seeking a wife?"

"I am, indeed, Your Highness. A wife who can bake gingerbread and who . . ."

"Oh no, I never bake gingerbread. But I am seeking

a husband. He must be as kind as he is handsome. He must know how to play on the slide trombone."

The king's mouth made an "O" like the hole in the heel of his stocking.

"I cannot play on the slide trombone," he said at last. "But I can shoot an arrow as straight as the tail of a comet." He took a deep breath.

"Then I'm sorry to hear that," said the princess. "The husband for me is the man who can play on the slide trombone."

253

Her smile made him wish he could say, "Yes, I can!" But all he could do was bow and take to his horse once again. He rode home with his chamberlain to brood.

Quite a long time passed. (A hole had now appeared in the heel of the king's other stocking. And he had never felt so lonely, besides!) One day he said, "Lord Chamberlain, it is plain to see that I must do without gingerbread."

"To tell you the truth," he said, "I like Princess Calliope best. She is not as beautiful, of course, as she is wise. But then, what chance have I, since I cannot play on the slide trombone?"

"As a matter of fact," the Lord Chamberlain said, "I was thinking of Princess Calliope, too. She is, as you say, very wise. Perhaps she knows what can be done."

"Excellent advice!" cried the king. "I shall go to see her at once."

Princess Calliope listened to the king. Then she said, "Let me think about this. I am sure we can come to some sort of agreement."

He paced up and down outside of her chamber. At last she came to the door.

"I have it," she said with a bow. "A husband should be as kind as he is handsome. That is better than one who can play on the slide trombone."

"And a wife should be wise," the king said quickly. "She does not need to know how to bake gingerbread."

They clasped hands together. Calliope said, "Then let us add something to our marriage vows. We must never again mention slide trombone . . ."

". . . or gingerbread!" The king finished with a laugh that shook the walls of the castle.

They lived happily together for nearly a year. They ruled their kingdom as well as anyone could.

Then one day everything went wrong. The king dropped the crown on his foot. The queen awoke with a headache. The Lord Chamberlain was ill. The cook slept late. The court painter put his head through Their Majesties' new portrait. The queen's dog chewed up all the paintbrushes. Outside, it snowed one minute and rained the next.

The king was angry; the queen was cross. They quarrelled all day.

"I wish," the king shouted, "that you could bake

gingerbread! Then SOMETHING would be right about this terrible day."

"And why," cried the queen, "can't YOU play on the slide trombone? It would certainly help to calm my nerves!"

They glared at each other with anger and spite. The forbidden words had been said. Their marriage vow was broken.

They both turned around and swept from the room to the opposite ends of their castle.

They stayed there for days feeling grumpy and sorry for themselves. Servants left food on trays near their doors, then scampered away before the doors might open.

The citizens of Mulligatawny were worried. "What has gone wrong at the castle?" they asked.

At last Queen Calliope looked at herself in her mirror. "The king married me because I was wise, not beautiful," she said. "Now, was it wise to shout SLIDE TROMBONE at him?"

It certainly was not. She sent for the Lord Chamberlain.

At the other end of the castle King Pilaf was trying to shave himself. "Oh, that nose and those eyes," he said to the king in the mirror. "You are not nearly so handsome as you like to believe."

He wiped blood from the cut on his chin. "Why, the queen married me because she thought I was kind! Was it kind to shout GINGERBREAD?"

He sent for the Lord Chamberlain.

Before very long, from one end of the castle came the odor of scorched pots. From the other came sounds like an elephant blowing its nose.

The servants rushed in one direction holding their ears. In the other they rushed holding their breath.

The citizens of Mulligatawny thought the world was coming to an end.

But then, in the middle of one night, the smells grew sweeter. At the very same time the sounds became more tuneful. The servants hurried about with noses high in the air to smell the delicious smells. They paused in their work to hear the sweet sounds. The citizens of Mulligatawny began to hope for the future.

At last the Lord Chamberlain made an announcement. Their Majesties would come from their opposite sides of the castle. They would meet in the Great Hall.

With a blast of trumpets, the door at one end of the Great Hall swung open. In marched the king with an apron around his middle. He had a baker's hat on his head and flour on his nose. He carried a pan of the most perfect gingerbread. It was the best that had ever

been baked in his kingdom—or in any other.

Without any sound at all the doors at the other end
of the Great Hall opened. Through them stepped the
queen. She raised a slide trombone to her lips. She
played such a melody that even the nightingales
hushed.

From that very day the first sound heard each
morning in Mulligatawny was Queen Calliope's slide
trombone. The first scent was that of King Pilaf's fresh
gingerbread. It became the custom of the citizens to
awake at sunrise to sniff and to listen. Their noses and
their ears would tell them if all was still well in the
kingdom.

To the end of their days they were never
disappointed.

Focus

1. What was King Pilaf looking for in a queen?
2. What three things did Calliope want in a husband? Which ones did King Pilaf have?
3. What agreement did Pilaf and Calliope make when they got married?
4. Why did King Pilaf finally learn how to bake gingergread?
5. Why did Calliope learn how to play the slide trombone?

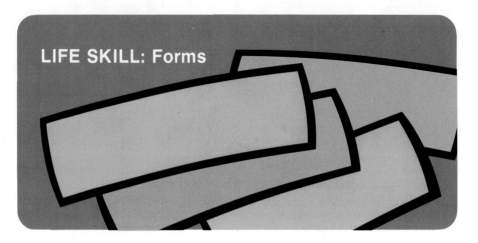

Queen Calliope wants to have a talent show. She needs people to act in the show. She also needs people to bring food. She wants people to help clean up after the show.

Queen Calliope hopes a lot of people will take part in the show. She needs a way to keep track of what each person is going to do. She has made up a form for people to fill in. It has blank spaces where people may write in what they want to do. King Pilaf is the first person to fill in the form.

1. Name: *King Pilaf*

2. In the show I will: *Tap dance*

3. I will bring: *Gingerbread*

4. I will help clean up after the show: (X)yes ( )no

The form tells the queen many things. It tells her that King Pilaf will tap dance in the show. It also tells her that he will bring gingerbread. How does she know if the king will clean up?

If your school had a talent show, you could use much the same form. It might look like one of these.

1. Name: *Jane Yee*
2. Grade: *4*
3. In the show I will: *Give a puppet show*
4. I will bring: *Cheese*
5. I will help clean up after the show: (X)yes ( )no

1. Name: *Juan Ramos*
2. Grade: *3*
3. In the show I will: *Play piano*
4. I will bring: *apples*
5. I will help clean up after the show: (X)yes ( )no

Now use what you have learned to answer these questions. Write the answers on your paper.

1. On which line do you write what you will do in the show?
2. If you want to bring oatmeal cookies, where do you write that?
3. On which line do you write your name?
4. If you are in the third grade, where should you write this on the form?
5. What do you do if you will help clean up?
6. Name some other times when you might fill out forms.

261

Gingerbread was King Pilaf's favorite food. Lots of people enjoy gingerbread—but not as many as enjoy pancakes!

PANCAKES AROUND THE WORLD

ELIZABETH VAN DORN

An Australian sits down to a plate of *pikelets* and jam. A Jamaican's mouth is watering. Why? Because he is soaking *bammee* in milk before he fries them. A Zuñi in New Mexico munches on *fry bread*. Did you ever think that each of those people is eating the same kind of food? What's more, you have eaten that food, too. What do you call it? That depends on where you live. *Johnnycakes* may be the name you use, or flapjacks. *Griddlecakes* is what some people call this food. Other people say *stacks o' wheat.* Many people call them *pancakes.* Pancakes are eaten the world over.

Visit a village in Mexico. You may hear the slap-slap sound of *tortillas* in the making. Water and salt are mixed with wheat or cornmeal to make the batter. Then these flat pancakes are cooked over a low fire. Sometimes they are eaten plain. Or they may be filled with meat or cheese. *Tortillas* are part of many Mexican meals.

From Mexico you can go south to South America. There you will find cowboys sitting around an open fire. They roll flour and water into little balls. Then they flatten them and poke tiny holes through each center. They are making *tortas fritas.* You would call them fried pancakes.

The people of France make pancakes, too. French pancakes are called *crepes*. The batter is made of flour, milk, eggs, salt, and oil. These very thin pancakes are cooked quickly in a hot pan. They can be used in hundreds of ways. *Crepes* may be rolled around mushrooms, meat, or fish. Then they may be topped with cheese or sauce and baked as a main course. There are also sweet dessert *crepes*. They may be filled with fruit or cheese. Served in a flaming pan, *crepes* are hard to resist!

In Israel, pancakes are called *latkes*. They are made with grated raw potatoes. They may be served with applesauce. Potato pancakes are eaten in Germany, too. There they are made with onion and parsley.

In some parts of Russia you could ask for a *pannkook*. You will get only one, but it will be as big as your plate! Spread on some jam—it's a real treat!

Many Russian dinners will include bite-sized pancakes. They are called *sirniki*. They are made with eggs, cottage cheese, and cream cheese. *Sirniki* can be eaten throughout the meal. Then comes dessert—heaps of light *blini*. These paper-thin pancakes are filled with cheese or fruit. A touch of sour cream goes on the top. In Finland, similar pancakes are rolled up with fruit preserves. The topping may be fresh peaches and honey.

Chapatis sizzle over a charcoal stove in India. They swell like small balloons. Flip! They are turned over and puff up again. Whack! The Indian cook flattens them and butters them. They are eaten with shellfish, or tomatoes and eggs. Other pancakes are served with a sweet and spicy coconut filling.

East of India lies China. Some Chinese pancakes are very thin. Sometimes they are filled with pork and eggs. At other times, the filling is slices of roast duck and sauces. In either case, they then are a food that can be eaten with the fingers. And in both cases, they are good!

In Italy, there is a tasty cousin of the pancake. Take leftover bread dough, stretch it, and whirl it around. Top it with tomato sauce. Then sprinkle on meat and vegetables and bake it. What have you got? Pizza!

You can see that people in most countries eat some kind of pancake. It may be a *crepe*. It may be a *pannkook*. The names and kinds of pancakes vary. But all over the world people eat pancakes.

Would you like to cook your own pancakes? This recipe is for a North American-style breakfast.

Basic Pancakes: (Makes about 12 five-inch pancakes)

$1\frac{1}{2}$ cups sifted white flour

$2\frac{1}{2}$ teaspoons baking powder

$\frac{3}{4}$ teaspoon salt

1 egg, well beaten

1 cup of milk

3 tablespoons salad oil

1. Sift flour, baking powder, and salt together.
2. Mix the egg, milk, and salt in another bowl.
3. Pour milk mixture into flour mixture. Stir only enough to get everything wet.
4. Cook on a hot griddle or frying pan. When cakes show bubbles on top, turn them to cook on the other side. Cooking should take about two minutes.
5. Serve with butter and maple syrup.

Focus
1. Pancakes have many names. Give three names they are called in different parts of the world.
2. Name two things that are put on pancakes when they are served as a main dish.
3. How else are pancakes served?
4. What is the main idea of this story?

Pizza, the story said, is a "tasty cousin" to the pancake.
Great-aunt Pippa has her very special version of pizza.

Great-aunt Pippa's Pepperoni Pizza

LEE BENNETT HOPKINS

Frederick was in a hurry to get to his Great-aunt Pippa's cottage. It was an important day for him. In honor of his tenth birthday, Great-aunt Pippa was preparing his favorite food—pepperoni pizza.

Frederick knew he shouldn't walk along Dragon Path to get to Great-aunt Pippa's cottage in the middle of the forest. But there were only two choices. He could walk down Sparta Road through Spartatown, which would take at least a half-hour longer. Or he could go along Dragon Path and hope he didn't meet any dragons. Frederick could hardly wait to taste Great-aunt Pippa's pizza. He decided to take Dragon Path.

As he walked, Frederick thought about his special birthday treat. Great-aunt Pippa was the only person in the land who knew how to prepare pepperoni pizza. And Great-aunt Pippa made it only on special occasions, like today.

Frederick hurried along Dragon Path. When he came to the row of great oaks he breathed a sigh of relief. Now he was only several minutes away from Great-aunt Pippa's cottage. But all at once he heard a thrashing noise. From behind the row of great oaks a huge green dragon stepped out. He lashed his great tail and blocked Dragon Path so that Frederick could go no farther.

"Oh, oh," thought Frederick. "This means trouble."

"Frederick, Frederick," the dragon said calmly, "you will be my dinner tonight. Frederick-food is my favorite. I'm so glad you came by here today."

Frederick trembled with fear.

"Frederick-food isn't very good," he said, his voice shaking. "You don't want me for dinner. Please don't eat me up!"

"But I'm hungry," said the dragon, "so very, very hungry. Today I'm especially hungry for Frederick-food. You will be my dinner. You should be pleased. Not all dragons like tough boys for their dinner. You should feel privileged that I've chosen you."

Frederick thought quickly. How could he get out of this? If he could only gain a little time.

He tried to sound calm. "All right, Dragon. If I must be your dinner, I must. But first I have to say good-by to my poor, old, dear Great-aunt Pippa. Her cottage is only minutes away. Allow me this chance to kiss her good-by forever and ever."

The dragon sat down under one of the great oaks. "Well, now," he said. "I'm not unreasonable. I'll let you go if you promise to go straight to Great-aunt Pippa's, kiss her good-by forever and ever, and then come right back. But don't try to trick me. I must have

Frederick-food for my dinner. If you care for your old aunt, you'll be back. Otherwise I'll come and get you. Then I'll have Frederick-food for my main course and Great-aunt Pippa for dessert!"

"I promise," Frederick said. "I'll come right back." Without another word he ran as fast as he could to the end of Dragon Path where Great-aunt Pippa's cottage stood.

"Frederick, Frederick," Great-aunt Pippa said when she saw her nephew. "Why do you look so whitened and frightened? Today is a special day. It's your birthday. Aren't you happy about the pepperoni pizza I've prepared for you?"

"Oh, yes," Frederick answered. "I'm happy to see you, Great-aunt Pippa. I'm happy it's my birthday. And you know how much I love your pepperoni pizza. It's the best pepperoni pizza in the whole, wide world. Everybody talks about your pepperoni pizza, Great-aunt Pippa. Everybody."

"You don't look very happy, Frederick," Great-aunt Pippa said.

"I do have some bad news," Frederick admitted. "Coming along Dragon Path, I met a dragon who asked me to go to dinner."

"Dinner?" asked Great-aunt Pippa. "Tonight? How can you go to dinner with a dragon tonight? I've made my perfect pepperoni pizza for your birthday!"

"Well," Frederick said, "the dragon wants me for his dinner. He wants to eat me up. If I don't go back soon he said he would come here. He'll eat me for the main course and you for dessert. I'm going back, Great-aunt Pippa. I just came to say good-by."

Frederick tried to be brave so Great-aunt Pippa wouldn't be alarmed, but she didn't look frightened at all. Instead, her eyes flashed angrily. "Come inside for a minute and let me fix something. I'll show that dragon a thing or two."

Frederick followed Great-aunt Pippa into her kitchen. She took a slice of pizza and popped it into her oven.

"Oh, that smells good," said Frederick, his mouth watering. "I can't wait to taste it."

When the pizza was done, Great-aunt Pippa took it out of the oven. Quickly, she sliced as many pieces of pepperoni as she could fit on it. She poured freshly ground pepper on top of the pepperoni. She added a handful of fiery chili peppers. Then she took her hottest homemade hot pepper sauce and poured it all over the pizza slice.

"How are you going to eat that?" Frederick asked.

"Easily," Great-aunt Pippa answered. "Like this."

She took the pizza slice and began to eat it as fast as

she could.

"May I have just one bite?" Frederick asked.

"Never! A bite of this and you won't be able to eat anything again. I'm used to hot stuff. This pizza is dragon insurance!"

Great-aunt Pippa finished the pizza and licked her fingers. "Now let's go," she said. "I have something to say to that dragon."

"Please don't go," Frederick begged Great-aunt Pippa. "Please! This dragon means business. He even knew my name. I'm the one he wants. If he eats you, too, no one ever again can taste your prized pepperoni

pizza. Think of that! Nothing could be worse, Great-aunt Pippa."

"Pepper and paprika!" Great-aunt Pippa replied. "I've dealt with dragons before. This one is no smarter than the others I've met."

Frederick saw that it was no use. Great-aunt Pippa was stubborn. The dragon would eat him and his great-aunt, too, and her famous pizza would be lost forever. He felt very sad.

They walked down Dragon Path to where the dragon waited. When he saw the two of them coming, the dragon danced around in a circle. He cried out, "Dinnertime, dinnertime! Double-dinner, double-dinner. Frederick-food for my main course and Great-aunt Pippa for dessert. This is my luckiest day!"

Frederick turned to Great-aunt Pippa. "Go back," he pleaded. "I told you not to come with me. I begged you. If the dragon eats you, no one ever again will have the privilege of tasting your prized pepperoni pizza!"

"Pepper and paprika again!" Great-aunt Pippa answered. "No dragon is going to eat me or my great-nephew—especially on his birthday. Leave this to me."

"Dinnertime, dinnertime. Double-dinner, double-dinner," babbled the dragon.

Great-aunt Pippa stared at the dragon. "You are not having Frederick, nor me, for your dinner," she said. "If you take one bite, one tiny chew or gnaw of my nephew, I'll destroy you."

"Ha!" said the dragon. "If you mess around with me, old woman, I'll breathe my deadly flames on you and toast you."

"Oh, you will, will you? Do you know who I am?" said Great-aunt Pippa. "I can breathe flames, too. Hotter than any flames you can breathe. Only a few hours ago I had seven dragons for my dinner—you will be the eighth. I'll make a nice pot of dragon stew out of you. What's more, I'll cook you with the flames from my breath!"

Great-aunt Pippa took a deep, deep breath. Her mouth was hot from the pepperoni, the freshly ground pepper, the handful of fiery chili peppers, her hottest homemade hot pepper and sauces. When she exhaled, peppered sparks flew out. Next came fireworks—pinwheels and rockets—and then long flashes of fiery flames.

The dragon's gigantic jaws dropped open. He began to shiver and shake, and his scales rattled. He stared at Great-aunt Pippa, unable to move.

"Who are you? What are you, old woman?" the dragon asked.

"Who am I? What am I? I am the dragon-eating woman of the woods," declared Great-aunt Pippa.

"The more dragons I eat, the more peppered sparks and fireworks, pinwheels and rockets, and long flashes of fiery flames shoot from my mouth."

Still unable to move, the dragon gazed in amazement at Great-aunt Pippa.

Great-aunt Pippa said, "With my next breath I'll fry you to a crisp. Then I'll have you as my eighth dragon-dinner course." She took another deep, deep, breath.

"No, no, no!" the dragon begged. He blinked twice and lashed his tail. Then he turned around and sped down Dragon Path. In seconds he was only a tiny speck.

"There!" Great-aunt Pippa said to Frederick, who was still staring after the dragon. "That dragon won't come around these parts again. Never! Now let's go home and have our pepperoni pizza in peace."

And they did. And the dragon never came back to Dragon Path again. Never!

Focus

1. Why was Frederick in a hurry to get to his Great-aunt Pippa's cottage?
2. What did he do that got him into trouble?
3. How did Frederick talk the dragon out of eating him?
4. Tell how Great-aunt Pippa outsmarted the dragon.

The Toaster

A silver-scaled Dragon with jaws flaming red
Sits at my elbow and toasts my bread.
I hand him fat slices, and then, one by one,
He hands them back when he sees they are done.

WILLIAM JAY SMITH

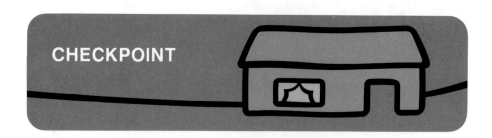

CHECKPOINT

**Vocabulary:
Word
Identification**

Write the five words below on your paper. Find the meaning of each word in the second list. Write the correct meaning next to each word.

1. trombone   people of a town or city
2. *crepes*   a blend of things
3. citizens   a musical instrument
4. cottage   very thin pancakes
5. mixture   a small house

**Vocabulary:
Vocabulary
Development
(context clues)**

Read the sentences. Pick the best meaning for each underlined word.

6. Carlos was <u>astounded</u> to find tacos in a store in Chicago. He thought they were made only in Mexico.

   <u>Astounded</u> means: unhappy   surprised   thoughtful

7. The dragon <u>cavorted</u> in the woods. He hopped and skipped around singing, ''Double-dinner!''

   <u>Cavorted</u> means: put on a bib   went to sleep   jumped for joy

Choose the word that best finishes each sentence.

8. Great-aunt Pippa was _____.
   frightened   clever   shy

9. The dragon was _____.
   generous   patient   scary

10. When Frederick saw the dragon he felt _____.
   brave   timid   sleepy

Many years later, Frederick's dragon had to fill out a form. This is what it looked like.

Name: *Dragon*
Address: *Short Oaks, Lizzard Lane*

Check one box by each item:	Like	Dislike	Don't Know
Peanut butter	X		
Gingerbread	X		
Mussels			X
Griddlecakes	X		
Pizza		XX	

11. Where does the dragon live now?
12. Which foods does the dragon like?
13. Which food is he still unsure of?
14. Why do you think he dislikes that one food?

Elisabeth, the Treasure Hunter

Felice Holman

he autumn wind had blown the people off the beach and given it back to the gulls and the terns. Along the shore, the tide had left little pools among the rocks and sand, and they reflected the fall sky coolly.

"Oh, look, Papa!" Elisabeth said. "The sky in the pool is full of starfish instead of stars."

"Quite true," said her father, looking into the pool. "Quite true." Then he gazed down the beach, following the line of brown seaweed and shells at the high-tide mark. He let his eyes take him way down the curve of the shore to the long jetty of rocks that went out into the water.

"There's nobody here at all," Elisabeth said, following his gaze. "Nobody, that is, except you and me, and that pirate out at the end of the rocks."

"What makes you think he's a pirate?" her father asked, looking out to the point where a man was fishing.

"Oh," Elisabeth replied, "he's only pretending to fish, you know. I've been watching him. He hasn't caught a thing. I'm sure he's a pirate, guarding his treasure."

285

A Plover

"Hmmm," said Papa. "Do you think it is hidden on this beach?"

"Absolutely!" said Elisabeth. She looked at him closely to see the effect of her idea.

"Oh, well, in that case . . ." began her father.

"In that case, I think we should hunt for it," said Elisabeth.

"How would you begin?" asked her father.

Elisabeth thought for a moment. "Well, I'd take my shovel and dig, mostly," she said.

"Hmmm," Papa said again. "I wonder if that's quite enough? You and I have no experience in this kind of thing."

"Yes," said Elisabeth with a frown. "That's true. If we could only get some experience!"

"Perhaps we could have a practice treasure-drill. Then we would be ready for the real treasure when we learn all the tricks. What do you think?"

The idea was outstanding! Elisabeth nodded vigorously and smiled with great pleasure.

"It's getting near lunchtime. Let's talk to your mother about this." Papa took Elisabeth's hand, and they started back over the sand. They climbed the sea wall, and then hurried down the road to the house.

As they entered the kitchen, Papa asked Mama, "Do you think you could pack us a treasure? Valuable, but not too valuable . . . in case we don't find it."

Mama looked confused for only a moment, and then she brightened right up and moved busily about the room.

"I can have it ready in five minutes," she said.

"Good," said Elisabeth.

"Fine," said Papa, with a hungry look.

They turned their backs and, in less than five minutes, Mama handed them a bright red tin box.

"Don't get your feet wet," she said.

When Elisabeth and her father returned to the beach, the tide was very low. There were a pair of ring-necked plover, very elegant in their dark necklaces. They were picking their way daintily along the shore, looking for something tasty.

"I believe," said Papa, "that the tide has ebbed as far as it is going to today." He looked at his watch. "Yes, right on the button! Low tide."

"You mean you can tell what time the tide will be low?" asked Elisabeth.

"Oh yes," Papa said. "The tide is as regular and as reliable as clockwork. With simple arithmetic we can tell at just what minute the tide will be high and low each day. But look, who is that?" Papa turned his attention to the figures of an extremely tall man and a very small boy who seemed very busy out at the sand bar.

"From his height and the cut of his coat, I think that's Professor Eckleberry," Papa said.

Elisabeth and her father walked down to the edge of the water, and waded through a shallow pool. Then they walked out onto the sand bar where, amid the long

grasses, Professor Eckleberry and the little boy were digging for clams.

"Good morning, Professor," Papa called out.

Professor Eckleberry stood up straight. His elegant, long black coat and the heavy, gold watch chain across his vest seemed to Elisabeth a strange costume for the beach. But she did not say so. She felt better when she looked at his feet. They were bare, and his trousers were rolled up to his knees.

"Ah, good day, good day," said Professor Eckleberry.

The little boy turned. He stared at Elisabeth in a way that was serious but friendly.

"What's that you're doing?" asked Elisabeth.

"Clamming," said the boy, digging in the sand with his bare toes.

"My grandson Charles and I are just digging a few clams to bring to Mrs. Eckleberry for lunch," the Professor said. "Watch!" He reached for a large stone and threw it down very hard on the wet sand. Immediately, a little fountain of water blew up into the air, next to the stone. The little boy fell to his knees and began to dig. There, just a bit below the surface, was a small clam.

"Why, he showed you where he was!" Elisabeth exclaimed. "Could I do it?"

"Of course," said Professor Eckleberry, bowing a bit. "Help yourself."

Elisabeth picked up a stone as large as she could lift and threw it onto the sand. Nothing happened.

"Either that wasn't hard enough or there's no one home down there," said Professor Eckleberry. "Try again over there."

Elisabeth threw the stone down again. Immediately a thin fountain blew up in the air. "There he is!" she cried. She dropped to her knees and dug with her fingers. "And here he is!" She held up the clam. Then she got a little water in her pail and carefully placed the clam on the bottom of it.

"That is a soft-shell clam," said Professor Eckleberry, "but that's just a manner of speaking. The shells aren't really soft so don't try putting your finger in one that's partly opened. They'll nip closed on you. That clam dug himself into the sand with a special foot he has. The sand protects him from the waves when the tide is in."

"Professor," Papa said, "I wonder if you could be of some assistance to us?"

"It would be my pleasure," said Professor Eckleberry. "We've got all the clams we need."

"Well," said Papa, "we've come down here to hunt for treasure." He held up the red tin box.

Professor Eckleberry raised his eyebrows and Charles looked up with interest. "I see," Professor Eckleberry said, and then he sighed. "So few people find real treasure. Of course, sometimes they just look in the wrong places for the wrong things."

"Have you ever found a real treasure?" Elisabeth asked eagerly.

"Often," Professor Eckleberry said. "Often . . . and always." And then he put his hand up to his chin and

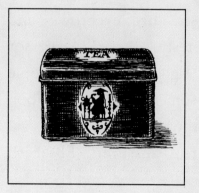

seemed to forget about Papa and Elisabeth.

"Of course, one of the best ways to find treasure," said Papa, getting Professor Eckleberry's attention again, "is to be sure there is one."

He held up the tin box again.

"Mmmm," is what Professor Eckleberry said.

"So," Papa went on, "it occurred to me that you might find it convenient to bury it for us. And then," Papa reached into his pocket and brought out a pencil and a piece of paper, "if you could just sketch us a simple map of its location or scribble a quick clue, we would be most grateful to you."

Professor Eckleberry looked at the box. "Well, I suppose that could be done. Yes, I suppose so." He picked up the box and started off down the beach.

"We'll keep busy around here," called Papa.

"Don't let the pirate see you," warned Elisabeth.

Charles was already busy at the end of the sand bar. He picked up a handful of soaking wet sand and let it dribble through his fingers to form beautiful designs. Then he let other dribbles pile up into little castles. Then he dribbled little turrets and ramparts. "Very soon," he said, "the water is going to come and flood this castle." He picked up a small mud snail that was going by and put it on top of the sand tower. "You know what else?"

"No, what?" asked Elisabeth.

"We are sitting on the bottom of the ocean."

Elisabeth thought about this. "My goodness, you're right!" she said. "Why, all of this," and she swept her arm toward the dark line of seaweed at the high-tide

mark, "will be the bottom of the ocean when the tide comes in."

A loud cry made her look up. A gull suddenly dipped down to the shore at the tide line. It grabbed something in its mouth, and then flew up high over the beach and dropped the something on the stones below.

"What is he doing?" asked Elisabeth.

Papa said, "He's found something good to eat that has a hard shell on it—perhaps a clam. But he can't crack the shell himself, so he drops it from a height onto the rocks."

"There he goes again," said Charles.

"Sometimes he has to drop the same shell several times," Papa explained. "And sometimes another gull will take it from him when it falls. Then there's an interesting chase to watch." The gull gave another loud cry.

"You know what the gulls call, don't you?" asked Charles, returning to his castle dribbling.

"No, what?" Elisabeth asked.

"They say, 'Cha-a-a-arles. Cha-a-a-arles!' Like that."

"Oh," Elisabeth said. "It must be nice to have all those birds calling you by your first name."

"Yes, it is, rather," said Charles.

Papa seemed a bit grumpy. "To tell you the truth,"

Calico Scallop

he said, "I always thought they were calling *my* name."

"What's his name?" Charles whispered to Elisabeth.

"Horace," said Elisabeth.

"Too bad," said Charles to Papa, "but they don't."

Papa frowned, but cheered up quickly as Professor Eckleberry reappeared at the edge of the sand bar, with a rather pleased look on his face and a little piece of paper in his hand. He gave the paper to Papa.

"This is the first clue," said Professor Eckleberry. "You'll find the others as you go. But," and he held up his hand in warning and looked at his watch, "they're only good for a little while—an hour or so."

"Why?" asked Elisabeth.

"Aha!" Professor Eckleberry replied, smiling a secret smile.

"Thank you for your help, Professor," said Papa. "Will you join us?"

"No, thank you, I can't," said Professor Eckleberry. "Mrs. Eckleberry is waiting for the clams. But perhaps Charles, here, would care for a bit of a treasure hunt. He might even come in handy on some of the clues. Very handy."

"Could he, Papa?" asked Elisabeth.

"By all means," Papa answered.

Charles picked the snail off the top of his castle and joined them.

"All right," Papa said, as Professor Eckleberry disappeared beyond the jetty. "Let's take a look at the clue."

Elisabeth and Charles came over to look and Papa read:

Three rocks near one rock,
Masqueraders dwell.
From house to house,
From shell to shell.

Elisabeth looked puzzled. Charles looked thoughtful. Papa looked annoyed. "I only asked him to make a little map. Well, come on! We might as well get going."

Papa led the way, frowning at the clue as he walked away from the sand bar. Elisabeth followed, carrying her pail and shovel. Charles brought up the rear, dragging the long clam rake his grandfather had been using.

"There is only one thing I can make of this clue," said Papa. "We will find something or other, in or near something, that is near three rocks, that are near one rock. Hmmm . . . well, that much is clear." He looked happier.

They walked along single file for a minute or so. Then Elisabeth called, "Papa, look! There are three big rocks right down at the edge of the water!"

Then Charles pointed and said, "And there's one

Mud Snails

rock all by itself farther up on the shore."

Elisabeth and Charles ran down to the edge of the water where the tide had exposed three large rocks. The rocks stood like mountains about a small pool of water. The water had belonged to the sea and had been left behind by the tide as it slowly left the shore. Now, for a little while, it was a separate pool. As Elisabeth and Charles peered in, they saw a strange sight.

"It's full of snails," said Elisabeth, "and they're walking around pretty fast."

Papa came up to the pool. "If they're walking around pretty fast, you'd better look at them again. The snails I know are very slow-moving."

"They look like snails," Charles said, "but they have awfully long legs."

"Aha!" said Papa leaning over the pool. "What you have discovered here is a very clever character called the hermit crab. And you're right about one thing. His shell once belonged to a snail. The hermit crab has no shell of his own, you see. So he borrows, or sometimes takes one, from a snail and uses it for a house."

"I guess he's only pretending to be a snail, then,"

said Elisabeth.

"Yes, I suppose you could say that," said Papa. "The hermit crab looks for a bigger shell every time he grows a bit. The shell he has now will get too tight for him. Then he'll have to find a new home."

Suddenly a bright look flashed over their faces.

"That's the clue!" cried Charles, hopping on one foot.

"That's the clue!" cried Elisabeth.

Hermit Crab

Papa whipped the paper out of his pocket. He read: " 'Three rocks near one rock.' Well, that's right, anyway. 'Masqueraders, dwell!' *Masqueraders?* Why, that's the . . ."

"That's the hermit crab!" cried Elisabeth. "He's dressed up like a snail!"

" 'From house to house,' " read Papa.

" 'From shell to shell!' " finished Elisabeth and Charles together.

"I used to have one for a pet," Papa said.

"Oh, Papa, I want to take one home!"

"Me, too," said Charles.

"Why, look at that!" exclaimed Elisabeth. "There's a piece of paper in the pool, partly hidden under a shell."

"A piece of paper!" Papa exclaimed. "That must be Professor Eckleberry's next clue."

Charles reached into the pool for the paper. "Look what happens when I touch the hermit crab," he said. And right before their eyes the crab seemed to disappear, slamming the door of the shell.

Papa laughed. "He uses his legs to make a door. Let's see the clue." He took the wet paper from Charles.

302

"What does it say?" asked Elisabeth.

"It says," Papa frowned:

*Thirteen paces
To shave men's faces*

"That's all?" Elisabeth asked.

"Not another word," said Papa. "Now really! And it's way past lunchtime."

"Well, let's shove off then," said Charles. "Standing here isn't finding us any treasure."

"Exactly where would you suggest we shove off to?" Papa asked.

"Let's just mosey along the shore until we get an idea," said Charles, and he began to mosey.

"Wait a minute," Papa said suddenly, becoming his old cheerful self again. "It does say 'Thirteen paces,' so if we're going to walk, we might as well count our steps."

Charles took the biggest steps that he could, and counted thirteen paces. Elisabeth counted her steps, but didn't get quite as far because she was walking behind Charles. Papa's paces took him farthest of all because his legs were the longest.

"All right now," Papa called, "let's each of us look around and see what he can see."

"I'm not a 'he,'" complained Elisabeth.

"That's just a form of speech," Papa said, stooping

over to examine the wet sand.

"What I have is shells," said Elisabeth. "Hundreds and hundreds of shells! All shapes and sizes and colors. They're beautiful!" She sat down and picked out the shells she liked best and dropped them into the bucket. "This one looks like a doll's fan," she said.

"That's a scallop," said Papa. "Some of them have lovely patterns on them."

"And this shell looks like one of the turrets on Charles's sand castle," said Elisabeth, holding it up.

"It's a wentletrap," Papa said, "but some people call it the staircase shell. You can see why."

"And look at this one, and this one. And this one looks like a little boat with a seat in it."

"Then it won't surprise you to know," said Papa, "that it is actually called a boat shell." He turned around and called, "What have you found, Charles?"

"This crab," Charles said. "He just came out of a hole right at my feet. And look at him! His claws don't match."

Papa and Elisabeth went over to look. It was a strange-looking creature. It had one small pinching claw and one large one which it carried crossed over in front of itself.

"Why, that old fellow is a fiddler crab," Papa said.

"Maybe they call him a fiddler because he carries his

claw like a violin," said Elisabeth.

"You're probably right," said Papa.

"And look at this one coming out from under the rock," said Charles. "He's green."

"He walks sideways," said Elisabeth

"Ah!" said Papa. "His body is green, but he's called the blue crab. See his blue legs. Most crabs walk sideways, I believe. And they all have to change their shells from time to time in order to grow. These blue crabs just slip out of their old shells and wait for a new one to grow. While they're out of their shells, we call them soft-shell crabs."

"If they're out of their shells, they have no shells at all. Right?" asked Elisabeth.

"Right!" said Papa.

"Then why don't we call them no-shell crabs?"

"Well," said Papa, and there was a long pause. Elisabeth smiled. There was always a certain pleasure in asking Papa a question he couldn't answer.

"What I suggest," Papa continued, "is this. Let us walk very slowly, between Charles's position here and my position up ahead. Let's see if we can find whatever it is that will shave men's faces."

They formed their line again and walked along, heads down, looking closely at the wet sand.

"See that rock?" Elisabeth pointed. "It was

uncovered when we were down here before. Now the water has come up over it."

"Tide's coming in," Papa said. "We'll have to hurry. Professor Eckleberry said the clues were good for only an hour, and I guess that's what his 'Aha!' meant. The tide will cover the clues pretty soon."

"Look at this funny, sharp shell sticking out of the sand," said Charles. "Oh, here's another."

"Here's another," said Elisabeth.

Blue Crab

"Aha!" said Papa, stooping suddenly and pulling one out of the sand. "Aha!"

"Aha, what?" asked Elisabeth.

"These clams are called razor clams. See, this is one of the empty shells. It's shaped just like an old-fashioned razor. Now here's what I was thinking . . ."

"Razors!" exclaimed Elisabeth.

"Exactly," said Papa.

"Razors!" exclaimed Charles.

"Exactly," said Elisabeth.

Papa uncrumpled the wet clue. " 'Thirteen paces to shave men's faces.' "

"Well, that's settled," said Charles.

And then Papa said, "Well, I never!"

"What is it?" Elisabeth asked.

"Look!" Papa exclaimed. "I was just turning over this razor-clam shell in my hand, and there . . . do you see what I see?"

"There's writing in it," said Charles.

"It's another clue!" cried Elisabeth.

"I'm inclined to think so," said Papa. He looked closely at the shell, and read:

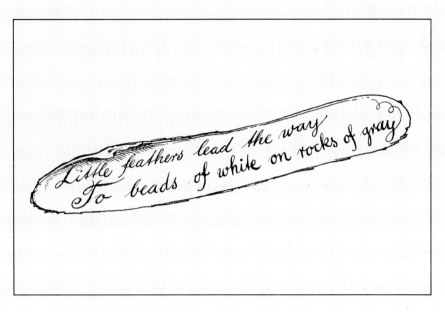

Little feathers lead the way
To beads of white on rocks of gray

Elisabeth said, "Papa, you're frowning again."

"Well, Eckleberry rankles me, that's all. No offense, Charles."

"No offense," said Charles.

"After all, this is my day off. I didn't expect to have to work so hard. And besides, I'm hungry."

"Charles and I can do this clue ourselves," said Elisabeth, taking pity on Papa. "Come on, Charles."

"Let me see the clue," said Charles, taking command.

"Can you read?" asked Elisabeth.

"Not actually," said Charles, "but looking at the writing helps me think."

Elisabeth and Charles stared at the clue as they wandered slowly up the beach.

309

"I'm getting hungry myself," said Elisabeth.

"I am, too," said Charles. Then he started walking in a way that reminded Elisabeth of a tightrope walker in the circus, putting one foot in front of the other and balancing with his arms.

"What are you doing?" she asked.

"I'm following the footsteps, see," he said.

Elisabeth looked down and saw the tracks in the wet sand.

"Gulls have made those tracks," said Papa, who would not be left behind, after all.

"They're very feathery footprints," said Elisabeth. "I'm going to take one home." And she very carefully took a bird track up in her shovel.

"Feathery!" exclaimed Charles. *Feathers!*

"Aha!" said Papa. "I think you have just discovered part of the clue."

" 'Little *feathers* lead the way . . .' " said Elisabeth, remembering the clue. "Oh, come on, let's follow them!"

They formed their line again. This time Elisabeth took the lead, holding the bird track on the shovel. Charles followed, carrying the pail. And in the rear came Papa, with Charles's clam rake over his shoulder.

The bird tracks led down the shore, right along the water's edge. In some places the water was lapping at the little prints.

"None too soon!" Papa said. "A few minutes from now the tide will erase these marks and spoil the clue. Old Professor Eckleberry was cutting it pretty close."

The trail led them right up to the stone jetty. Charles and Elisabeth climbed up onto the nearest of the large rocks.

"The rocks are slippery," said Elisabeth.

"It's those reddish weeds that are so wet and

Irish Moss

slippery," said Papa. "They're called Irish moss."

"There's a pool of starfish in the weeds," Elisabeth said.

"That's the place they are most at home," said Papa. "A place that is wet most of the time suits them best. Look at the rocks above us. You can see the clear lines of color that mark the layers of rock, uncovered by the tide for different lengths of time. The things that need the sea the most live at the bottom. The strongest, like the periwinkles, live on the top because they have learned to live without the sea. The periwinkles are those small, brownish-gray snails. They live in the crevices of the rocks, where they are covered only by the highest tides and wet by the spray. Below them are the layers of plants and animals that must be in the sea longer each day in order to live."

"The layer above us is all blue," Elisabeth said.

"Those are mussels," Charles said. "Grandpa and I sometimes gather them."

"There are so many of them," Elisabeth said. "What keeps them from falling off the rocks?"

"They make a little thread that holds them on tight," said Papa. "And they can move up the rocks a little at a time by making new threads."

"The layer above that is all brown seaweed," Elisabeth said.

"I see a white layer," said Charles. He started to climb farther up the rocks and a little farther out on the jetty.

"Look!" Charles called. "The rocks are covered with thousands of little white cabbages. Ow! They're sharp!"

"They look like beads to me," said Elisabeth, who had followed him.

"Aha!" exclaimed Papa. "Beads! What kind of beads did you have in mind?"

"White beads," said Elisabeth.

" 'Beads of white,' " Papa said.

" 'Rocks of gray,' " Charles added.

"The clue!" cried Elisabeth. "The clue!"

"But what are beads doing here on the rock?" asked Charles.

"Well," Papa said, puffing out a bit as he did when he knew the right answer, "although these *look* like beads, or tiny cabbages, they are really a small animal called a barnacle."

"An animal!" exclaimed Elisabeth. "How can they be alive? They're so hard and they look so empty!"

"Some of them are empty," Papa agreed. "But many of them are closed up tightly over a little, upside-down animal that is waiting for the sea to come back. Many things on the rocks look different when the sea comes and covers them. The rockweeds float instead of hanging as they do now. Those blue mussels open up and start to eat. The barnacles unfold and reach out of their shells, with their feet, for food, though they can never move from the place they have chosen to grow. They are fastened so tightly that even the wildest waves can't wash them away."

"There are barnacles on this rope, too," Charles said.

"Barnacles attach themselves to lots of things—even to the bottoms of ships," said Papa. "That rope is probably used to tie up a boat sometimes."

"There's no boat here now," said Charles and he tugged on the rope.

"But there is *something* on it," said Elisabeth, and

she went over to help Charles pull. "Maybe it's a fish."

"Not likely," said Papa. "Not likely."

Suddenly what was on the end of the rope came into view.

"Papa!" cried Elisabeth. "Charles! It's our tin box! It's the treasure! The treasure is tied to the end of this rope!"

And there it was . . . the tin box that Mama had packed. Charles and Elisabeth climbed down to the

edge of the rocks, amid the red moss. They pulled the box out of the water.

"Why, that rascal Eckleberry!" Papa exclaimed. "The idea of putting our treasure in the water!"

"Maybe he didn't put it in the water," Elisabeth said.

"Maybe the tide came up over it," said Charles.

"Oh, let's see what's in the box!" Elisabeth cried, hopping on one foot and trying to pry open the cover at the same time.

"Here, let me help," Papa said. "There!"

Inside the box everything was dry as could be, and there was the treasure, looking absolutely marvelous! There were large chunks of gold, looking like beautiful peaches. There were pieces of jade and amethyst, looking like bunches of grapes shining in the sun. There were rare jewels, looking like red, yellow and green hard candies. And there was a great big piece of chocolate frosted cake, looking like a great big piece of chocolate frosted cake.

"Oh, Papa," Elisabeth cried. "Of all the treasures we could find right now, this is the best!" She started to reach into the box, but stopped suddenly and held it out to her father. "Have some treasure, Papa," she said.

"Thank you," Papa said, taking a peach.

"Have some treasure, Charles," Elisabeth said.

Starfish

"Thank you," said Charles, and he broke off a chunk of chocolate cake.

Elisabeth took a bunch of grapes, and they all sat down on the rocks to eat.

"Mama is really a fine treasure packer," said Papa, trying the cake. "Really fine!"

Elisabeth and Charles nodded, and sampled some of the jewels.

"Look down at the end of the rocks," Elisabeth said. "The pirate is packing his fishing things. If he goes away and stops guarding his treasure, perhaps we will be able to find it . . . now that we have the experience."

"Hmmm," said Papa.

"My feet are getting wet," Elisabeth said.

"The tide is coming in quickly now," said Papa. "We'd better be moving off the rocks," and he led them down onto the sand.

"But, Papa," protested Elisabeth, "we can't leave without the pirate's treasure. We've eaten the one we found, and now we have no treasure to take home."

Papa looked at Elisabeth, thoughtfully, and then at the pail in her hand.

"Oh, haven't we now!" he said, putting his hand into the pail and poking the hermit crab and the starfish and the periwinkles.

Elisabeth looked down at the pail. "Why, it *is* a kind of treasure, isn't it?" She smiled, and picked up the shovel with the gull's track on it.

Charles peered into the pail, too. The mud snail from his castle was now settled snugly in the sand among the shells and seaweed. "Do you suppose *this* is

Limpets

what he was guarding?" Charles asked, glancing at the pirate.

"Perhaps," Papa said. "Perhaps not so much *guarding* as *watching*."

Elisabeth looked down to the point of the rocks where the terns were diving for fish and the gulls were screaming. She looked down at her feet, where the water was running back onto the shore, gathering in the little pools and all the creatures it had left for a while. She stamped very hard and a little clam blew her a fountain.

"And you know what?" Elisabeth said. "There's *lots* more treasure for next time."

GLOSSARY

Full pronunciation key*   The pronunciation of each word is shown just after the word, in this way: **ab·bre·vi·ate** (ə brē′vē āt).

The letters and signs used are pronounced as in the words below.

The mark ′ is placed after a syllable with primary or heavy accent, as in the example above.

The mark ′ after a syllable shows a secondary or lighter accent, as in **ab·bre·vi·a·tion** (ə brē′vē ā′shən).

a	hat, cap	k	kind, seek	ŦH	then, smooth
ā	age, face	l	land, coal	u	cup, butter
ä	father, far	m	me, am	u̇	full, put
b	bad, rob	n	no, in	ü	rule, move
ch	child, much	ng	long, bring	v	very, save
d	did, red	o	hot, rock	w	will, woman
e	let, best	ō	open, go	y	young, yet
ē	equal, be	ô	order, all	z	zero, breeze
ėr	term, learn	oi	oil, voice	zh	measure, seizure
f	fat, if	ou	house, out	ə	represents:
g	go, bag	p	paper, cup		a in about
h	he, how	r	run, try		e in taken
i	it, pin	s	say, yes		i in pencil
ī	ice, five	sh	she, rush		o in lemon
j	jam, enjoy	t	tell, it		u in circus
		th	thin, both		

---

*Pronunciation Key and respellings are from *Scott, Foresman Intermediate Dictionary* by E. L. Thorndike and Clarence L. Barnhart. Copyright © 1979 by Scott, Foresman and Company. Reprinted by permission.

A

a·part·ment (ə pärt′mənt) *noun.* a room or group of rooms in which to live: We moved into a three-bedroom *apartment.*

ap·ple·sauce (ap′əl sôs′) *noun.* sliced apples cooked until soft, often with water and spices added.

ar·e·a (er′ē ə or ar′ē ə) *noun.* 1. territory or region. 2. amount of surface: Let's prepare this *area* for a vegetable garden.

ar·gu·ment (är′gyə mənt) *noun.* 1. the reasons for or against something: The firefighter's *argument* for a new engine was accepted by most of the townspeople. 2. a discussion had by persons who do not agree.

ar·rive (ə rīv′) *verb.* to reach or come to a place: The guests were *arriving* at eight o'clock.

B

band·age (ban′dij) *noun.* strips of cloth or other material used to cover a wound or injury. —*adjective.* having to do with bandages: *bandage* cloths.

barn·yard (bärn′yärd′) *noun.* the area around a barn used for the animals.

bas·ket (bas′kit) *noun.* 1. a container made of twigs, grass, plastic, or strips of wood woven together. 2. the amount a basket holds.

bat·ter (bat′ər) *noun.* a mixture made of flour, milk, and eggs that is cooked to make muffins, cake, or pancakes.

bay (bā) *noun.* an inlet in a sea or lake, usually larger than a cove: A *bay* is a safe place to anchor small boats.

be·have (bi hāv′) *verb.* to act correctly; to do what is right. **behaved, behaving.**

be·neath (bi nēth′) *preposition.* 1. under; underneath; below. 2. not worthy of.

Ben·ja·min (ben′jə mən) *noun.* a male name.

ber·ry (ber′ē) *noun.* a small, juicy fruit having many seeds. **berries.**

blan·ket (blang′kit) *noun.* a soft bed cover woven from wool, cotton, or other material. **blankets.**

bleat (blēt) *verb.* to make the sound of a goat, sheep, or calf. **bleated, bleating.** —*noun.* the sound made by a goat, sheep, or calf.

bounce (bouns) *verb.* 1. to jump or spring into the air like a ball. 2. to cause to bounce.

bug·gy (bug′ē) *noun.* 1. a light carriage drawn by a horse. 2. a baby carriage. **buggies.**

bus·y (biz′ē) *adjective.* 1. to have plenty to do. 2. in use. 3. full of activity. **busier, busiest.**

323

C

calm (käm or kälm) *adjective.* 1. free from noise or activity; still; quiet. 2. peaceful: The *calm* nurse treated the screaming child.

can·dle (kan'dl) *noun.* a stick of wax with a wick, used to give light.

Car·o·line (kar'ə līn) *noun.* a female name.

car·pen·ter (kär'pən tər) *noun.* someone who builds and repairs wooden parts of houses, barns, or ships.

cav·ern (kav'ərn) *noun.* a large space in the ground; a big cave: It was dark and damp in the *cavern.*

cer·tain·ly (sėrt'n lē) *adverb.* with no doubt; surely: I will *certainly* be in school tomorrow.

cham·ber·lain (chăm'bər lən) *noun.* the person who manages a king's household.

Char·lotte (shär'lət) *noun.* a female name.

Chi·na·town (chī'nə toun') *noun.* a special section of a city where persons of Chinese background live.

chis·el (chiz'əl) *noun.* a sharp tool used for cutting and chipping wood, metal, or stone.

cir·cus (sėr'kəs) *noun.* a traveling show of animals, acrobats, and clowns. —*adjective.* having to do with the circus: a *circus* clown.

cit·i·zen (sit'ə zən) *noun.* 1. a person who by birth or choice is a member of a nation. 2. a person who lives in a town or city.

com·fort·a·ble (kum'fər tə bəl) *adjective.* 1. free from pain: The patient was more *comfortable* after the nurse changed the bandage. 2. having comfort; at ease.

cot·tage (kot'ij) *noun.* 1. a small house: The servants lived in a *cottage* on the large estate. 2. a summer home at a vacation area. **cottages.**

cou·ple (kup'əl) *noun.* 1. a few items that go together: She bought a *couple* of new dresses. 2. a man and a woman who are married, engaged, or dancing together.

crepe (krāp) *noun.* thin pancakes made in France, usually served rolled around a filling. **crepes.**

curve (kėrv) *noun.* 1. a line that has no straight part. 2. something that has the shape of a curve; a bend. **curves.**

D

de·bate (di bāt') *noun.* discussion or argument for or against a certain question or subject. —*verb.* to argue for or against something; consider; discuss: Franklin was *debating* whether or not to buy a new bicycle. **debated, debating.**

de·feat (di fēt') *verb.* 1. to make fail. 2. to overcome: Our team will *defeat* the other team in baseball.

de·li·cious (di lish'əs) *adjective.* satisfying to the taste or smell: The homemade soup was *delicious.*

de·liv·er (di liv'ər) *verb.* 1. to distribute or give out: The mail carrier *delivered* the mail early today. 2. to give forth in words, as a speech. **delivered, delivering.**

de·liv·er·y (di liv'ər ē) *adjective.* having to do with bringing objects to people: The *delivery* van brought the flowers.

de·part·ment (di pärt'mənt) *noun.* a branch or division of something larger: the police *department.*

de·scribe (di skrīb') *verb.* to tell or write about something: This book *describes* what the Grand Canyon looks like. **described, describing.**

des·ert (dez'ərt) *noun.* a sandy area with no water and no trees.

de·sign (di zīn') *noun.* the arrangement of details, such as color and shape, in a work of art: The dress had an attractive *design* on it.

des·sert (di zėrt') *noun.* the course served at the end of a meal such as ice cream or fruit.

dou·ble (dub'əl) *adjective.* twice as many or twice as much: I had a *double* serving of peas.

drag·on (drag'ən) *noun.* a large, fierce imaginary animal that looks like a winged snake, breathing out fire and smoke; often a character in old stories.

E

earn (ėrn) *verb.* 1. to win; to get as deserved. 2. to be paid in return for work done: Tom wanted to *earn* enough money to buy a book.

ech·o (ek'ō) *noun.* a sound that is repeated. **echoes.**

eighth (ātth) *adjective.* the next one after the seventh: the *eighth* grade. —*noun.* one of eight equal parts.

en·gine (en'jən) *noun.* a machine that uses fuel to make motion and power: a car's *engine.*

325

en·joy (en joi') *verb.* to be happy with; to take pleasure in: Our family *enjoyed* a trip to the beach. **enjoyed, enjoying.**

e·quip·ment (i kwip'mənt) *noun.* things that are needed; supplies: Our camping *equipment* included sleeping bags and tents.

es·pe·cial·ly (e spesh'ə lē) *adverb.* more so than others; particularly: This dictionary is written *especially* for children.

ex·cite (ek sīt') *verb.* 1. to stir up the feelings of. 2. to cause to be stirred up or aroused: The noisy crowd *excited* the horse in the parade. **excited, exciting.**

ex·tra (ek'strə) *adjective.* something beyond what is expected; additional.

F

fac·tor·y (fak'tər ē) *noun.* a building in which items are made by machines or by hand. **factories.**

fa·vor·ite (fā'vər it) *adjective.* liked best: Red is my *favorite* color.

fern (fėrn) *noun.* a type of plant that has feather-like leaves, but no flowers or seeds.

fe·ver (fē'vər) *noun.* a higher than normal body temperature, that is, above 98.6°F (37°C).

flake (flāk) *noun.* a small, thin, flat piece of matter: a *flake* of snow. **flakes.**

fla·vor (flā'vər) *noun.* 1. a particular taste. 2. something used to season food or drink.

for·ev·er (fər ev'ər) *adverb.* never ending; always.

for·got·ten (fər got'n) *verb.* past tense of **forget;** failed to remember; failed to do: I have *forgotten* my math book. **forget, forgotten, forgetting.**

for·ward (fôr'wərd) *adverb.* 1. toward the front; ahead. 2. to the front.

fos·sil (fos'əl) *noun.* a hardened trace of the remains of animals or plants from long ago. **fossils.**

Frank·lin (frangk'lən) *noun.* 1. a male name. 2. often a family or second name: Benjamin *Franklin.*

Fred·er·ick (fred'ər ik) *noun.* a male name.

fret (fret) *verb.* to worry or be unhappy about something: The farmers *fretted* about the dry weather. **fretted, fretting.**

fright·en (frīt'n) *verb.* to make or become afraid or scared: The puppy was *frightened* by the thunder.

fruit (früt) *noun.* the juicy product of a tree, bush, or shrub, that has a seed and a cover.

fur·ni·ture (fėr′nə chər) *noun.* items for a house, such as beds, chairs, tables, and couches.

G

ga·rage (gə räzh′ or gə räj′) *noun.* 1. a shop for repairing cars. 2. a building in which one can keep a car. —*adjective.* having to do with a garage: a *garage* door.

get (get) *verb.* 1. to come to have; to obtain; to receive: Our neighbors have *gotten* a new sail boat. 2. to prepare. 3. to catch hold of. **got, got** or **gotten, getting.**

Gil·les·pie (gə les′pē) *noun.* 1. a male name. 2. a last name.

gin·ger·bread (jin′jər bred′) *noun.* a type of cake made with ginger and molasses.

gleam·ing (glē′ming) *adjective.* reflecting light; polished; shiny.

got·ten (got′n) *verb. See* **get.**

gray (grā) *adjective.* the color that is a combination of black and white. —*noun.* a horse that is gray in color.

groom (grüm or grum) *verb.* to feed and take care of a horse. **groomed, grooming.**

guest (gest) *noun.* a person staying with others in a home or hotel or motel; a visitor: Aunt Maria was our *guest* for the weekend.

H

hos·pi·tal (hos′pi təl) *noun.* a place in which the sick or injured are cared for.

Hu·bert (hyü′bərt) *noun.* a male name.

hud·dle (hud′l) *verb.* to crowd close together: The kittens *huddled* together to keep warm. **huddled, huddling.**

I

im·print (im′print) *noun.* a mark or impression made by pressure: You can make an *imprint* in the mud with your foot.

J

Jan·u·ar·y (jan′yü er′ē) *noun.* the first month of the year, coming before February.

jew·el·er (jü′ə lər) *noun.* a person who makes, sells, or repairs jewelry.

jew·el·ry (jü′əl rē) *noun.* any earring, necklace, bracelet, or ring made to be worn; often set with gems.

Ju·ly (jủ lī′) *noun.* the seventh month of the year, coming between June and August.

K

ket·tle (ket′l) *noun.* a metal container for cooking, especially for boiling water or other liquids: The campers cooked stew in a *kettle.*

kiln (kil or kiln) *noun.* an oven or furnace used for burning, baking, or drying: The clay pots were fired in the *kiln.*

L

lan·guage (lang′gwij) *noun.* 1. the words spoken and written by humans. 2. the speech of one nation. —*adjective.* having to do with a language: a French *language* school.

laugh·ter (laf′tər) *noun.* 1. the act of laughing. 2. the sound a person makes when happy.

Lib·er·ty (lib′ər tē) *adjective.* a type of circus horse that can walk on its back legs and stop quickly when galloping.

like·ly (līk′lē) *adverb.* probably: I shall *likely* be at the pool on a hot day.

loose (lüs) *adjective.* not shut up or tied: The dog got *loose* and wandered away. **looser, loosest.**

M

mam·mal (mam′əl) *noun.* one of a group of warm-blooded animals that has a backbone: Cats and dogs are *mammals.*

mane (mān) *noun.* the long, heavy hair on or around the neck of a horse or lion.

mar·riage (mar′ij) *noun.* 1. married life. 2. the wedding ceremony. —*adjective.* having to do with marriage and the act of marrying: a *marriage* ceremony.

mar·ry (mar′ē) *verb.* 1. to join as husband and wife. 2. to take as husband and wife. 3. to become married: The man and woman were *married* on Sunday. **married, marrying.**

mer·ri·ly (mer′ə lē) *adverb.* in a cheerful way; laughing and joyful: We ran *merrily* through the snow.

met·al (met′l) *noun.* any material such as iron, gold, copper, or silver that has a shiny surface and can be melted and hammered into a thin sheet or stretched into wires.

Mex·i·co (mĕk'sə kō) *noun.* a country in North America, south of the United States and north of Guatemala.

mil·lion (mil'yən) *adjective.* one thousand thousands; 1,000,000.

min·er·al (min'ər əl) *noun.* any substance not plant or animal, found by digging in the earth: Rocks are *minerals*. **minerals.**

mix·ture (miks'chər) *noun.* 1. things that have been stirred or blended together. 2. a mixing: Biscuits are a *mixture* of flour, salt, baking powder, and water.

moan (mōn) *verb.* 1. to make a sound of pain. 2. to complain. —*noun.* a low, long sound made in pain or grief: The sick puppy gave a low *moan*.

moss (môs) *noun.* a small, soft green or brown plant that grows close to the ground or on rocks and trees: Soft green *moss* covered the bottom of the oak tree.

mur·al (myûr'əl) *noun.* a picture painted on the wall of a building, inside or out.

mus·sel (mus'əl) *noun.* a bluish-black shellfish, similar to a clam, found in both salt and fresh water.

N

neck·lace (nek'lis) *noun.* a string of jewels, gold, or silver worn around the neck: My grandmother has several pearl *necklaces*. **necklaces.**

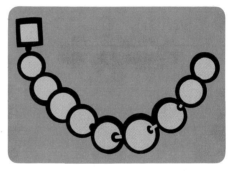

nurse (nėrs) *noun.* a person who is trained to care for sick or injured people. —*verb.* to care for sick people; to act as a nurse.

O

om·e·let (om'lit) *noun.* a dish made of beaten eggs fried and folded over, sometimes served with a filling. **omelets.**

on·ion (un'yən) *noun.* a sharp tasting and smelling vegetable with a bulb that can be eaten raw or cooked: Peeling *onions* can make your eyes water. **onions.**

op·po·site (op'ə zit) *adjective.* as different as two things can be: Left and right are *opposite* directions.

P

pack·age (pak′ij) *noun.* a bundle wrapped for carrying: The *packages* would not fit into the mailbox. —*verb.* to form into a bundle. **packages.**

pan·try (pan′trē) *noun.* a small room in or near the kitchen where food, dishes, or utensils are kept. **pantries.**

pas·sen·ger (pas′n jər) *noun.* a traveler in a train, bus, or plane, often paying money to travel. **passengers.**

pat·i·o (pat′ē ō) *noun.* 1. an outside terrace for sitting. 2. an inner courtyard that has no roof.

pil·low (pil′ō) *noun.* a soft cushion used to support the head while resting or sleeping: I use a feather *pillow* when I sleep.

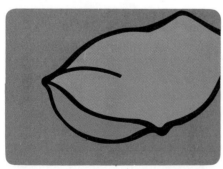

pol·ish (pol′ish) *verb.* to make smooth and shiny by rubbing: Jack *polished* the furniture. **polished, polishing.**

po·ny (pō′nē) *noun.* a type of small horse. **ponies.**

por·cu·pine (pôr′kyə pīn) *noun.* an animal covered with quills. **porcupines.**

pow·er·ful (pou′ər fəl) *adjective.* having power; strong, mighty: The *powerful* waves knocked the swimmers over.

pre·pare (pri per′ or pri par′) *verb.* make ready: The chef will *prepare* dinner. **prepared, preparing.**

priv·i·lege (priv′ə lij) *noun.* a special right; an advantage. —**privileged** *adjective.* having a special right or advantage: I feel *privileged* to have been chosen for this honor.

prob·a·bly (prob′ə blē) *adverb.* more likely than not: Caroline will *probably* ride the pony in the parade.

Q

quar·ter (kwôr′tər) *noun.* 1. one of four equal pieces: Each of the four of us had one *quarter* of the pie. 2. a coin equal to twenty-five cents.

quill (kwil) *noun.* 1. a long sharp hair on the body and tail of a porcupine. 2. a pen made from the stem of a feather. **quills.**

R

rein (rān) *noun.* a long narrow strip attached to a bridle, used to guide and control an animal: Bill held the *reins* tightly as he jumped his pony over the fence. **reins.**

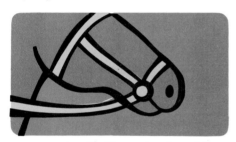

res·cue (res′kyü) *verb.* to aid or save from danger. **rescued, rescuing.** —*adjective.* having to do with saving someone or something: a *rescue* team.

re·tire (ri tīr′) *verb.* 1. to give up a job or occupation, especially because of age: Many workers *retire* at the age of 70. 2. to go to bed. **retired, retiring.**

route (rüt or rout) *noun.* 1. a regular course of a person making deliveries or sales: a newspaper *route.* 2. a road.

Rus·sia (rush′ə) *noun.* a country extending from Eastern Europe across northern Asia.

S

sad·dle (sad′l) *noun.* a seat for the rider on a horse's back or bicycle. **saddled, saddling.** —*verb.* to put a saddle on a horse. —*adjective.* having to do with a saddle: a *saddle* blanket.

safe·ty (sāf′tē) *noun.* lack of or freedom from danger: The young child ran to the *safety* of his mother's arms.

sci·en·tist (sī′ən tist) *noun.* a person that has a lot of knowledge in a field of science. **scientists.**

seam·stress (sēm′stris) *noun.* a woman who sews to earn a living. **seamstresses.**

Sep·tem·ber (sep tem′bər) *noun.* the ninth month of the year, coming between August and October.

ser·i·ous (sir′ē əs) *adjective.* 1. deep in thought; grave: He had a *serious* expression on his face. 2. important. 3. not fooling; honest; sincere. —*adverb.*

serv·ant (sėr′vənt) *noun.* a person who works in another person's household: Wealthy persons often have *servants.* **servants.**

sev·en·ty (sev′ən tē) *noun.* seven times ten; 70: Grandfather retired at the age of *seventy.* **seventies.**

shad·ow (shad′ō) *noun.* 1. shade made by a person, animal, or thing: The *shadow* of the building appeared large. 2. partial darkness.

shov·el (shuv'əl) *noun.* a tool with a wide scoop to lift material, especially dirt. —*verb.* to use a shovel; to lift and throw material. **shoveled, shoveling.**

sil·ver (sil'vər) *noun.* 1. a precious shiny white metal: The jeweler made a ring out of *silver.* 2. coins made from silver. 3. eating utensils made from silver.

sin·gle (sing'gəl) *adjective.* 1. just one: Teresa ate a *single* piece of pie. 2. for one thing or person. 3. not married.

snow·plow (snō'plou') *noun.* a machine that clears snow from streets, driveways, or railroad tracks.

squir·rel (skwėr'əl) *noun.* a small bushy-tailed animal that lives in trees.

straight (strāt) *adjective.* 1. not bent or curved: The road to the lake was *straight* and narrow. 2. going in a line.

stu·dent (stüd'nt or styüd'nt) *noun.* one who studies; a pupil: There are ten *students* in my reading group. **students.**

suc·ceed (sək sēd') *verb.* to do well; to turn out well: Sarah *succeeded* in learning a new language. **succeeded, succeeding.**

sug·gest (səg jest') *verb.* to propose or offer an idea: Ella *suggested* that the girls attend the movies. **suggested, suggesting.**

T

tel·e·vi·sion (tel'ə vizh'ən) *noun.* a device on which pictures may be seen and sounds may be heard.

Ter·e·sa (tə rē'sə) *noun.* a female name.

though (ᵵHō) *conjunction.* in spite of the fact: Even *though* it was snowing, we went to school.

to·ma·to (tə mā'tō or tə mä'tō) *noun.* a juicy red or yellow fruit eaten cooked or raw, often used in salads. **tomatoes.**

tor·til·la (tôr tē'yə) *noun.* a thin, flat, round cake made from cornmeal cooked on a flat surface and served hot. **tortillas.**

tour (tur) *verb.* 1. to travel; to take a long journey. 2. to walk around in. —*adjective.* having to do with traveling or touring: a *tour* guide.

tour·ist (tur'ist) *noun.* a person who is traveling for enjoyment; a traveler.

trom·bone (trom bōn′) *noun.* a brass wind instrument, played by sliding a piece of metal up and down to change the pitch.

tur·quoise (tėr′koiz or tėr′kwoiz) *noun.* 1. a greenish-blue stone used in jewelry: The bracelet is made of silver and *turquoise.* 2. a greenish-blue color.

U

un·com·mon (un kom′ən) *adjective.* not common; unusual; different.

un·der·ground (un′dər ground′) *adverb.* beneath the surface of the earth. —*adjective.*

un·pack (un pak′) *verb.* to take out of a trunk or container: John will *unpack* his suitcase.

u·su·al·ly (yü′zhü ə lē) *adverb.* in the usual way; commonly: *Usually* we roast a turkey for Thanksgiving dinner.

V

veg·e·ta·ble (vej′ə tə bəl) *noun.* 1. any plant whose fruit or other part is used for food. 2. the part of the plant used for food: Squash is my favorite *vegetable.* 3. any plant.

vol·un·teer (vol′ən tir′) *verb.* to offer a service for no pay. —*noun.* one who works without pay. —*adjective.* made up of or having to do with volunteers.

W

wade (wād) *verb.* 1. to walk through snow or water or something else that makes walking difficult: The tourists had to *wade* through cold water to look for clams. 2. to go through with difficulty, as a book. **waded, wading.**

whis·tle (hwis′əl) *noun.* 1. a device for making clear, shrill sounds: The coach used a *whistle* to call the team together. 2. the sound made by such a thing.

win·dow·pane (win′dō pān′) *noun.* a piece of glass in a window: John hit a baseball through the *windowpane* and broke it.

wood·chuck (wùd′chuk′) *noun.* an animal with a thick body and bushy tail that lives in North America; a groundhog. **woodchucks.**

wood·en (wùd′n) *adjective.* made out of wood.

Z

Zu·ñi (zü′nyē) *noun.* a member of the Pueblo tribe living in New Mexico. —**Zuñi** or **Zuñis** *plural.*

333

(Acknowledgments continued from page 2)

Reprinted by permission of Faber and Faber Ltd from *The Collected Poems of Theodore Roethke*.

Garrad Publishing Company for "Linda Richards" by David R. Collins. Adapted from "Four Women of Courage", edited by Bennett Wayne, reprinted with the permission of Garrard Publishing Co., Champaign, Illinois.

Florence Parry Heide for her poem "Rocks." Copyright © 1969 by Florence Parry Heide. Reprinted by permission of the author.

Scholastic Inc. for the poem "The Silent Cat" by David Kherdian from *Country Cat, City Cat*. Copyright © 1978 by David Kherdian and Nonny H. Kherdian. By permission of Four Winds Press, a division of Scholastic Inc.

William Jay Smith for his poem "The Toaster." From *Laughing Time*, published by Atlantic-Little, Brown, 1955, copyright © 1953, 1955, William Jay Smith. Reprinted by permission of William Jay Smith.

Toni Strassman for the poem "Before You Came This Way" from *Before You Came This Way* by Byrd Baylor. Published by Elsevier-Dutton in 1969. Text copyright 1969 by Byrd Baylor. Illustration copyright 1969 by Tom Bahti. Permission of Toni Strassman, Agent.

Albert Whitman & Company for the adaptation of "Great-aunt Pippa's Pepperoni Pizza" by Lee Bennett Hopkins. Reprinted with the permission of Albert Whitman & Company from *Monsters, Ghoulies and Creepy Creatures* selected by Lee Bennett Hopkins. Copyright © 1977 by Lee Bennett Hopkins. Also for "Mary Jo's Grandmother" by Janice May Udry. Adapted from *Mary Jo's Grandmother* © 1970 by Janice May Udry.

Reprinted with permission of Albert Whitman & Company.

World's Work Ltd, England, for "Bear Mouse in Winter," adapted text from *Bear Mouse* by Berniece Freschet, published in the UK and British Commonwealth by World's Work Ltd. Used by permission. Also for "The Queen Who Couldn't Bake Gingerbread," adapted text from *The Queen Who Couldn't Bake Gingerbread* by Dorothy Van Woerkom, published in the UK and British Commonwealth by World's Work Ltd. Used by permission.

Illustrators and Photographers: Peter Bradford, cover, 8–9, 84–95, 144–145, 148–149, 218–219; Gary Fujiwara, cover, 8–9, 46–47, 84–85, 148–149, 218–219; Richard Louie, 1, 3–7, 34–35, 44–45, 60–61, 82–83, 100–101, 112–113, 132–133, 146–147, 162–163, 184–185, 200–201, 216–217, 234–235, 246–247, 260–261, 280–281; Michael L. Pateman, 10–22, 62–81, 196–199, 236–245, 262–267; Robert Brower, 23–29; Murals courtesy of TWA, Los Angeles International Airport, 30–33; Lonnie Browning, 30–33; Jerry Pinkney, 36–43, 48–59; Don Weller, 86–99, 102–105, 134–143; Stephen Ogilvy, 106–109, 169; Linda Post, 110–111; David Cain, 114–127; John Kaufmann, 128–131; Rob Sauber, 150–161; Aliki, 164–168; Mary Anne McLean, 170–183; Glenna Lang, 202–215; Roseanne Litzinger, 220–233; Erik Blegvad, 282–321; William McDade 324–333.

Design, Ginn Reading Program:
Creative Director: Peter Bradford
Art Director: Gary Fujiwara
Design Coordinator: Anne Todd
Design: Lorraine Johnson, Linda Post, Kevin Young, Cathy Bennett, Kristen Dietrich